Praise for *Customer Magic*

"Leaders at Macquarie understand that magic follows from the dedicated pursuit of customer experience excellence! In this book, Joseph A. Michelli, a consultant and author who has worked with The Ritz-Carlton Hotel Company and Macquarie, crafts another invaluable resource for organizations of all sizes to create repeat business and referrals. Bravo to the leaders at Macquarie. Much success to you as you master these powerful lessons and craft your *Customer Magic*."

Horst Schulze, Co-founder of The Ritz-Carlton Hotel Company and bestselling author of *Excellence Wins*.

"From my roles as a Chief Experience Officer, coach to the C-suite, speaker, and author, I know firsthand the importance of creating a human-centric culture. I also know the challenge of executing a strategy that gets the most from your people, process, and technology. In *Customer Magic*, my friend and colleague, Joseph A. Michelli artfully captures how an Australian technology company creates world-class customer experiences in keeping with the company's purpose—'to make a difference for markets that are overcharged and underserved.' Most importantly, Joseph shows you how to drive repeat business and referrals! So, what are you waiting for? Isn't it time to master the magic?"

Jeanne Bliss, Founder and President of Customer Bliss, Co-founder of the Customer Experience Professionals Association, and bestselling author of books including *Chief Customer Officer* and *Would You Do That to Your Mother?*

"Macquarie Technology is an example of customer problem-solving and customer care. Through that unwavering customer focus, Macquarie delivers impressive returns to shareholders. *Customer Magic* explains how the founders, David and Aidan Tudehope, and other leaders ask the right questions and deliver what they call 'personal accountable service.' This important book lays bare what superior customer experience requires and how rewarding it is for staff and shareholders as well."

Robert McLean AM, Co-author of *The Imperfectionists* and *Bulletproof Problem\Solving*, former Dean of the Australian Graduate School of Management and Director Emeritus of McKinsey & Company.

"Who would have thought a humble, unconventional Aussie brand had so much magic to share? Michelli has thoroughly and elegantly captured the story of Macquarie Technology in a way that helps leaders and business owners believe in what is seemingly impossible at times. Building strong relationships, perseverance in service training, and the commitment to untiring service storytelling are just some of the tactics that Michelli reports from the practical magic that delivers extraordinary customer experiences. Another brilliant business case unpacked and a dose of inspiration to any business leader or customer experience leader who wishes to succeed in gaining global attention and competitive advantage."

Jaquie Scammell, Founder and CEO of ServiceQ and author of *Service Mindset* and *Service Habits*

CUSTOMER MAGIC

CUSTOMER MAGIC

THE macquarie WAY

How to reimagine customer experience to transform your business

JOSEPH A. MICHELLI

BLACK STONE PUBLISHING

Published in 2024 by Blackstone Publishing
Cover design by Tess McCabe
Photo by Matt Nelson on Unsplash
Internal design by Production Works

Printed in the United States of America

ISBN 979-8-8746-3110-9
Business & Economics / Customer Relations

Version 1

Blackstone Publishing
31 Mistletoe Rd.
Ashland, OR 97520

www.BlackstonePublishing.com

This book is dedicated to everyone who strives to reimagine customer experience.

Contents

Foreword

The history of business management is filled with examples of industry-leading companies that either lost their premier market position or ceased to exist altogether. Case studies of companies like Polaroid, Blockbuster, Enron, and even IBM spotlight how hard-earned success is precarious and difficult to sustain.

For decades, I've researched, taught, and written about the challenges leaders face in managing innovation and stewarding change within successful businesses. My perspective, which I call "ambidextrous leadership," encourages leaders and managers to address two distinct challenges simultaneously. First, continually improve the ability to compete over the short term by ensuring strategy, structure, people, culture, and processes all work in harmony. Second, spark revolutionary innovation and drive organizational change.

This book, *Customer Magic*, provides an insightful deep dive into Macquarie Technology Group, a company founded by students of mine at the Harvard Business School: David and Aidan Tudehope. David and Aidan's commitment to lifelong learning, disruptive and iterative innovation and operational excellence has resulted in three decades of steady success for Macquarie – a challenger brand in the rapidly changing technology and telecommunication sectors.

Throughout the years, Macquarie has earned prestigious customer experience and industry rewards, but unfortunately, the company's leadership strengths have remained largely under the radar. As someone who has closely watched this renegade Australian brand succeed for decades, I am delighted that Joseph Michelli chose to adeptly share Macquarie's revolutionary lessons with you.

In the pages ahead, Joseph, a #1 *New York Times* best-selling author and globally recognized customer experience consultant, takes you on an in-depth journey into Macquarie's remarkable and unconventional approach to customer experience, innovation, and consistent growth.

Customer Magic shows you how to leverage effective customer listening to produce engagement, repeat business, and customer referrals. It provides stories of Macquarie's exceptional customer service delivery while also offering tools for driving positive storytelling across your organization.

Packed with actionable insights, *Customer Magic* is a case study of what is possible when leaders have a deep sense of purpose and a commitment to creating value for customers and markets that are underserved and overcharged. Joseph's keen analysis and inviting writing style also highlight Macquarie's disciplined and unique approach to innovating ideas that are optimized for the needs of core customer segments.

In short, *Customer Magic* is a must-read leadership book and a go-to resource for anyone seeking to create a purposeful culture that succeeds over the short and long term by producing world-class customer experiences and timely, customer-centric innovation.

What are you waiting for? It's time to dive into *Customer Magic*!

Michael L. Tushman, Ph.D.
Baker Foundation Professor
Paul R. Lawrence Professor Emeritus
Harvard Business School

Chapter 1

Macquarie's Customer Magic

Carol Moseley Braun states, "Magic lies in challenging what seems impossible." By that definition, this book is about business *magic*.

The company on center stage for this performance – Macquarie Technology Group, which I will refer to as "Macquarie" throughout the book – consistently *challenges* industries known for poor treatment of customers and monopolistic practices. While Macquarie may not be a household name, it is a successful "challenger" brand that has disruptively achieved *seemingly impossible* customer-centric results. The magicians – two brothers and an aligned team of leaders and frontline colleagues – have honed their craft in pursuit of a transformative purpose: "to make a difference for markets that are underserved and overcharged."

Despite minimal start-up capital and harsh competition from large, established brands, Macquarie's magic has produced a telecom, cloud, and cybersecurity business with stock values that have increased more than tenfold in the last decade alone. Macquarie earns countless rave reviews from loyal customers across global and regional brands.

Daniel Hawkins, the Australia/New Zealand Chief Information Officer for Domino's Pizza (a multinational pizza chain with over 19,500 stores in 90 markets), notes:

> "Macquarie is a valued strategic partner. They have consistently exceeded our service expectations and improved the effectiveness and efficiency of our systems. Through our relationship with Macquarie, we've reduced customer friction and improved our overall Domino's experience."

Matt Slade-Smith, the Group ICT Manager at Life-Healthcare (a leading independent medical device distributor), shares:

> "Having first engaged with Macquarie in 2007, our journey, much like theirs, has evolved. One thing that has never wavered is their focus on outstanding experiences. It is refreshing to see a partner so on top of customer service. With the most seamless migrations to Azure and our current environment now decluttered, much more scalable, robust, and cheaper, working with Macquarie is an absolute no-brainer."

Hayden Slee, Information Technology Infrastructure Manager at Fleetwood (an offsite manufacturer of modular construction and recreational vehicle solutions), notes:

> "Without access to Macquarie's resources, skills, and expertise, it would have taken years to reach this level of maturity and capitalize on our goals. They've become an extension of our team, and we have weekly meetings where engineers, project managers, and network administrators collaborate and work through issues. This has been great for skills sharing and ensuring nothing slips through the cracks. Macquarie even takes the time to send people to remote locations. Once, they sent a team member 1,242.7 miles north of Perth to scope a project. None of the vendors we've dealt with over the past five years have shown that commitment. The service provided by Macquarie's local team has accelerated IT support, which will advance business goals for years to come."

Similarly, Darrin Leggett, Executive Manager of Information and Office Services at Avivo (a homecare service company), shares:

> "We signed on with Macquarie Telecom almost two years ago, and I can tell you the honeymoon hasn't ended. From the word 'go,' Macquarie Telecom has exceeded my expectations, from outstanding project implementation to continually going above and beyond what was required."

Are Daniel, Matt, Hayden, and Darrin discussing a telecom and technology company?

From skeptic to advocate

When I heard about Macquarie many years ago, I doubted that a telecom and technology company was delivering transformative customer experiences. As a customer experience consultant who's worked with and written about world-class customer experience brands such as The Ritz-Carlton Hotel Company, Mercedes-Benz, Starbucks, and Zappos, it was *seemingly impossible* that a telecom company would authentically care for and about customers. However, data suggests Macquarie is a disruptor that challenges the seemingly impossible.

Like the rest of the world, Australia's telecom and technology sector is riddled with customer service issues. From 2017 to 2019, the Australian Telecommunications Industry Ombudsman logged approximately 153,000 formal customer complaints yearly. That's substantial in a country of roughly 25 million people. Those telecom complaints were roughly twice the number received in the banking sector. In the same period, Macquarie received an average of two minor complaints yearly.

Similarly, the Australian Communications Consumer Action Network (ACCAN) reported that the average Australian telecommunications customer spent 1.2 hours waiting in a phone queue before reaching someone who could help them. By contrast, Macquarie call centers average a 26-second wait time. MaritzCX's audit concluded that Macquarie Cloud Services outperformed MaritzCX's global norms and exceeded the information technology industry average on virtually every customer experience competency.

Not only is it unprecedented for a telecom or technology company to be a customer experience leader, but it's also unusual for an Australian company (as opposed to a US, European or Asian brand) to garner global attention as an outstanding service provider. However, after a decade of tracking Macquarie and gaining access to the company's inner workings, I've gone from skeptic to advocate, and I feel compelled to share the secrets behind their magic.

Intended audience

Before you join me on this Australian adventure, let's ensure this journey is right for you.

Customer Magic is written for difference-makers and innovators! Technology and telecom leaders will naturally gravitate to this book, but its lessons are applicable across country borders and industry sectors. *Customer Magic* also speaks to entrepreneurs and team members of businesses of all sizes at every organizational level (C-suite, owner, manager, frontline).

However, this book is *not* intended for passive readers. This book is designed to spark discussion and action. *Customer Magic* is an extension of Macquarie's previously mentioned purpose: "to make a difference for markets that are underserved and overcharged."

The success of *Customer Magic* hinges on you leveraging insights and tools to make a difference for those you serve. If you are willing to elevate your people, processes, products, technologies, and services, *the magic awaits.*

Context and accomplishments

For context, it's best to consider Macquarie as a single company with four aligned business units. While a brief and non-technical description of each division is provided here, Chapter 5 will offer a more in-depth look at how Macquarie's business units work independently and interdependently to create robust customer solutions and overarching company results.

Macquarie started as Macquarie Telecom in 1992. The Telecom business unit provides data, voice, mobile, and internet services to medium and large business customers. Macquarie Cloud Services provides comprehensive software as a service (SaaS) solutions and cloud resources ranging from colocation to private and public cloud. Macquarie Government provides cybersecurity to 42 percent of Australian government departments, protecting them against viruses and hackers. Macquarie Data Centres operates large data facilities where the cloud lives and also services clients from across Macquarie as well as large wholesale customers.

Collectively, Macquarie is globally recognized for leadership, innovation, customer experience excellence, and employee engagement. Rather than providing a lengthy list of achievements that Macquarie has accrued over its three-decade history, here are a few representative accolades.

Total Telecom is an organization that serves more than 250,000 senior executives, tracks telecom and technology trends, and recognizes industry leaders and innovators. In 22 years of Total Telecom's World Communication Awards, *no* Australian company had received an honor. That changed in 2020 when Macquarie won two World Communication Awards: Best Customer Experience (CX) and CEO of the Year (going to Macquarie's co-founder and CEO David Tudehope).

The CX award was conferred by David Homer, Senior Client Partner at Capita, who explained, "Providing the best all-round experience with customers is the focus for this particular award. The winner motivated staff to look for ways to delight customers hence increasing the company's net promoter score." In the context of the CEO of the Year award, Nokia UK and Ireland CEO Cormac Whelan said:

> "For the CEO of the Year, we're definitely looking for the X-factor and we definitely found it here. The judges described the winner as the most customer-experience-focused CEO they've ever seen . . . he championed increased competition in his own domestic market and has delivered outstanding growth for the company he himself founded in 1992."

In addition to leadership and customer experience recognition, Macquarie has been acknowledged as a Great Place to Work. Citing Macquarie's commitment to team member assessments, coaching, and training, the *Australian Financial Review* emphasized that Macquarie's leadership drives a highly engaged and inclusive workplace.

The following chapters will help you understand and apply Macquarie's award-winning approach to leadership, customer experience, innovation, and employee engagement. It includes:

- an inspiring company purpose and values,
- customer experience excellence based on a holistic model of people, real-time transparent measurement, optimized processes and systems, and customer-centric storytelling,
- competitive differentiation based on "zigging when others zag,"
- innovation fueled by a "Noah's Ark" methodology,

- a leadership model of freedom within boundaries and a founder's mentality that permeates the organization.

Before I detail the approach, let's preview what you will learn from this unconventional brand.

What's in it for you?

Consistent with Macquarie's commitment to delivering customer value, your study of Macquarie's business magic will provide practical insights on how to:

- identify customer pain points,
- develop solutions that remove customer pain,
- leverage a compelling unique value proposition geared to your target audience,
- create and sustain a customer experience culture,
- attract and select customer service talent,
- grow and retain subject matter experts who consistently demonstrate service professionalism,
- measure customer experience delivery,
- set, measure, track, and incentivize mission-critical business goals,
- inspire, align, and engage team members,
- evaluate emerging trends and determine their applicability to your customer segments,
- innovate solutions that meet your customers' stated and unstated needs,
- maintain a growth mindset and leave a legacy of business and customer success.

Maximizing your experience

Let's preview this book's layout so that you will get the most from *Customer Magic*. This nine-chapter book consists of the following:

- This context-setting chapter,
- Seven content chapters addressing customer experience, innovation, and leadership themes,
- A summary chapter that looks at Macquarie's future and your application of *Customer Magic*.

This book will present foundational concepts and strategies that have guided Macquarie during exponential growth, economic downturn, recovery, and transformation. These concepts are presented in language consistent with Macquarie's culture and reflect the importance of focusing on team members' and customers' evolving wants, needs, and desires. The goal of this book is to provide tools for your personal and business development. *Customer Magic* can be used individually, in team discussions, and with business book clubs.

In subsequent chapters, sections referred to as "Practice your magic" offer opportunities to reflect on, discuss, and apply Macquarie's best practices. At the end of each chapter, you will find a summary of key takeaways in a "Make your difference" section.

Customer magic in action

Before revealing Macquarie's insights and techniques, here are three examples of the company's service magic.

Like everything at Macquarie, the first story begins and ends with customer service. This time the service was directed to an Administrative Supervisor at a non-profit service provider, a prominent mental health and disability organization. The organization had recently migrated their mobile phones to Macquarie Telecom, and the Administrative Supervisor placed an after-hours call to make a provisioning change. On the receiving end of that call was a Macquarie Project Manager – Clinton Donovan. Clinton swiftly and professionally managed the request. This would mark the end of the service story at most companies, but *not* at Macquarie. Clinton elevated the service experience when he learned that the client had accidentally locked herself out of her office while completing the Macquarie call.

Since her keys and wallet were in her office, Clinton arranged an Uber, which he paid for from his personal account. Upon arriving home safely, she contacted Clinton to express appreciation and reimburse him. Clinton responded, "The only payment required is to know that you finish the night with a good meal and a nice glass of wine." The client had the final word, however, by sending a letter of appreciation to Macquarie leadership, noting:

> "I can't recall a time when someone I've dealt with professionally went all out to put my safety and well-being first and in no way made me feel like it was done out of obligation. There's a standard of customer service I think we all recognize as acceptable, but this encounter was beyond anything I would have expected from a provider given my predicament was not of a work nature."

These unexpected or seemingly implausible behaviors are expected at Macquarie, as evidenced by a service interaction with another customer – the Royal Australasian College of Surgeons (RACS). RACS was formed in 1927 and is a non-profit organization that trains surgeons and maintains surgical standards in Australia and New Zealand. On a Friday afternoon, as RACS was moving to a new office in New Zealand, RACS team members contacted Macquarie with a substantial and unexpected connectivity concern. Four Macquarie team members – Janet Blair, Maria Meyer, Saulius Kazlauskas, and Kate Larson – assessed RACS's issue and determined they needed a new router. To avoid business disruption, that router must also be delivered and brought online before Monday morning. Unfortunately, no courier could get the equipment to New Zealand that quickly. Working together, the Macquarie team *challenged the seemingly impossible.* Kate coordinated the team. Saulius offered expert technical support. Maria worked through the night to resolve a surprise from New Zealand customs. Janet adjusted her plans for the weekend to hop on a three-hour Saturday night flight from Australia to New Zealand.

Thanks to Macquarie's extraordinary team effort, RACS was fully operational from their new headquarters in Wellington, New Zealand, at the start of business on Monday morning. If that wasn't enough, Janet found time to take RACS team members to breakfast.

Let's close this chapter by showing how Macquarie team members helped a customer avert disaster. The customer was Rocky Bay, a 90-year-old community service organization based in Perth that provides disability support services. In a conversation, Michael Tait, Rocky Bay's Managing Director and CEO, credited Macquarie with helping his organization keep its essential services operating. Specifically, Michael noted:

> "Rocky Bay was attacked with a crypto lock, and from the moment that threat surfaced, we were anxious and uncertain about its likely impact. We'd heard stories of other organizations like ours closing because they didn't have the resources to pay the ransom. Macquarie, a trusted 20-year partner, jumped into action with astonishing speed, not wasting time discussing compensation or requesting purchase orders. Their team took charge in partnership with our IT team. Macquarie helped us stay confident and maintain positive morale throughout the operational disruption. Fortunately, no customer data was affected, and no information was extracted. More importantly, we were able to come through the challenge strong and resolved."

Dan Morgan, a Macquarie Personal Customer Technical Officer who worked on the team that responded to Rocky Bay's crisis, told me:

> "We are used to working in situations of heightened intensity and strive to empathize with the emotional impact these challenges pose for our customers and for those they serve. In the case of Rocky Bay, we were acutely aware that we needed to help Rocky Bay so they could serve their vulnerable customers."

Michael acknowledged the extraordinary level of empathy demonstrated by the Macquarie team:

> "We are fortunate to have many solid partners – most of whom do their job without our oversight – but Macquarie is different. Macquarie makes us better, and they are extensions of our team. Our Macquarie partners appear to genuinely care about us and our customers. Thanks to Macquarie's authentic support and concern, we can assist and create independent living opportunities for people like Mal Burgess."

Mal is a 61-year-old man paralyzed at age 22 after an automobile accident when he drove while being alcohol-impaired. A long-term resident of Rocky Bay, Mal has worked with Rocky Bay's rehabilitation specialists and speech therapists so he can speak to youth about the perils of operating an automobile after drinking. (For a video of Mal sharing his powerful message, please visit macquariemagic.com.au.) Michael adds that thanks to exceptional partners like Macquarie, Rocky Bay is fortunate to serve people like Mal, who in turn positively touch countless lives.

These types of customer service stories – along with many more that will be provided throughout the book – go *well* beyond the norm for telecom and technology providers. Frankly, they exceed service delivery standards for most businesses (even those in the hospitality sector). However, they are the way things get done at Macquarie.

Now that you've witnessed some Macquarie magic, it's time to dive deeply into the company's customer experience and innovation wizardry.

Chapter 2

David (and Aidan) Against Goliath

"Magic is pretty simple: It comes down to training, practice, and experimentation, followed up by ridiculous pursuit and relentless perseverance."
David Blaine

The biblical story of David and Goliath is rich with themes of courage, unwavering belief, and a *challenge to the seemingly impossible.*

While on a less epic scale, our story involves the challengers – brothers David and Aidan Tudehope, co-founders of Macquarie – battling a nearly 100-year-old, government-owned telecom giant. Before we get into lessons you can learn from the underdogs' struggle and details on how they triumphed, let's set the scene.

David and his younger brother Aidan were born, raised, and educated in Sydney. Both earned bachelor's degrees in commerce from the University of New South Wales. As Aidan completed his degree in the early 1990s, David was well into his professional career. David notes:

> "After graduation, like many of my peers, I went directly into the booming banking sector. During my tenure as a banker, I learned a lot about business and myself. For example, my greatest fulfillment came from providing direct service to customers in medium-to-large businesses."

Five years into David's career, as the banking industry was in a substantial recession, he closely tracked the Australian government's deregulation of the telecom sector.

Much like the break-up of the Bell System ("Ma Bell") in the US about a decade earlier, Australia's telecom monopoly faced parliamentary inquiries due to widespread service breakdowns and allegations that poor phone service caused business closures. The Australian Labor Party (ALP) government, recognizing the growing importance of the telecommunications sector to the economy, introduced a second licensed carrier, Optus Communications (which began operations in 1992), to rival the government-owned telecom Telstra, creating a duopoly in domestic and international services. The government then granted mobile licenses to Telstra, Optus, and a third competitor, Vodafone, creating a triopoly in mobile services.

David and Aidan launched Macquarie in 1992 (then known as Macquarie Telecom) at ages 25 and 20, respectively, and the company was in full swing by 1993.

Funded only by savings and unused holiday leave accrued during David's banking career, the brothers leveraged service passion and David's contacts to compete with the government-owned Telstra and new market entrants Optus and Vodafone.

In challenging the legacy telecom, David explains how Macquarie got its name:

> "When we started our company, we chose Macquarie because it reflected how we saw ourselves. We were reimagining a tired, impersonal, and seemingly uncaring government monopoly and aspired to improve our industry so people would want to be customers or employees. So, we looked for a name that spoke to our aspirations, as well as one that was proudly Australian. We chose Macquarie as Lachlan Macquarie was a "founding father" who transformed our country into a place where people wanted to immigrate and not one viewed as a prison farm for convicts. It was Lachlan Macquarie who recommended our country be named Australia."

David shares a personal experience of transformation, too: "Many of my friends wondered why I would leave a safe banking job for the uncertainties of launching a telecom company." Fueled by the optimism of youth and having no mortgages or outstanding financial obligations, David and Aidan seized their entrepreneurial opportunity, guided by Macquarie's purpose to make a difference in underserved and overcharged markets.

By 1993, Telstra struggled with a negative service reputation, voluminous customer complaints, and high-profile lawsuits from small business owners who referred to themselves as Casualties of Telecom (COT). David notes:

> "Telstra's problems were all over the media. People were upset about poor treatment and annual price increases, even as Telstra's costs decreased. Before crafting our offerings, I reached out to my former bank customers to assess the gap between their expectations and what they received from Telstra. Thanks to that input, our value proposition crystallized.
>
> "We first differentiated ourselves through clear and transparent billing. Our customers didn't get the traditional Telstra one-line bill that said 'pay this amount;' instead, they received all their call charges itemized and graphed. Our second differentiator was a laser focus on medium-to-large businesses. Before the age of the internet and mobile phones, this primarily involved helping companies with data they sent down phone lines and through faxes. Our third differentiator was service. Our primary competitor viewed customers as 'subscribers' and provided *no* service to account managers. We, however, viewed customers as people who deserved timely access to service professionals who would help them run their businesses smoothly."

While Macquarie's unique value proposition starkly contrasted with its primary competitors', success was far from guaranteed. David describes the company's early days as a time for learning and personal sacrifice. On the learning side, David notes:

> "When I first reached out to prospective customers from my list of former bank clients, I expected

Macquarie's early adopters would be people with whom I'd built the strongest relationships. To my surprise, that was *not* the case. Instead, we were much more successful selling to prospects who experienced the most pain with their existing telecom provider. Our value proposition was far more important than the strength of pre-existing relationships.

"Also, while my banking experience strengthened my understanding of business, I needed to improve my sales skills. People approached me with their banking needs and I presented product options. At Macquarie, we had to go to them and overcome their fear of changing to an untested provider. Customers had to trust that Macquarie would deliver on our promises and that choosing us wouldn't jeopardize their corporate careers. Since we were in a sell-or-die mode, I attended large sales workshops conducted by international trainers."

Once Macquarie secured its first group of customers, satisfied clients told their colleagues and the company grew steadily through referrals like this one provided by Dan Beeston, ICT Manager of Infrastructure at the Hall & Prior Health and Aged Care Group: "It's the people and the team that set Macquarie Telecom apart. When we've requested modifications, they listened, adapted, and took the feedback on board."

On the early sacrifice front, Aidan notes, "There isn't a role in our business that David and I haven't performed ourselves – whether that was selling, billing, taking bills to the post office or banking checks."

David adds, "We bought assemble-it-yourself office furniture and put that together on weekends. We functioned as corporate lawyers, HR leaders, and administrative staff. Those experiences helped us empathize with the challenges involved in those roles."

Since airfares were prohibitively expensive, David recalls traveling by bus to meet clients:

> "After working in Sydney, I'd change out of my business suit and into my tracksuit. I would then catch the Firefly coach for a nine-hour ride to Melbourne. We'd stop at The Big Merino (a 50-foot high, 95-ton rock sculpture of a sheep) in Goulburn and get a midnight dinner nearby. We'd arrive in Melbourne at dawn, and I'd change back into my business suit for that day's work. By nightfall, I'd be getting back on the bus for my return trip to Sydney."

Despite David and Aidan's sacrifices, customer acquisition was hampered by the company's financial limitations and the relative financial strength of its competitors. David notes:

> "Being a banker, I knew the importance of creating a business plan and financial forecast. However, Macquarie's early days taught me that *no* plan survives first contact. Our spreadsheet didn't track neatly with our plan, and we needed to make a profit from every customer we served. Without those profits, we couldn't care for future customers. In our early years, we had to turn away prospects who wanted discounts to switch to us. We could only do so much from a price perspective and maintain our service levels."

Additional external threats emerged as Macquarie's success garnered the attention of Telstra. David said:

> "There were periods when Telstra spent millions of dollars on lawyers to crush us – and frankly, the rest of the telecom industry. Since we offered a long-distance option and Telstra controlled the last mile of service, they would deploy tactics some referred to as 'deny, delay, and degrade.' It was as if Telstra was a Death Star that would send legions of stormtroopers to destroy competitors on far-flung planets. Those fighters didn't hesitate to fire their laser blasters.
>
> "Fortunately, they weren't as effective as people thought they would be. The telco wars often involved court battles over regulations designed to block the growth of competition. Many telecom companies left the business, but we navigated through those challenges and adapted accordingly, always staying true to our service value proposition."

Practice your magic

Typically, "Practice your magic" is presented twice per chapter. Questions are derived from content in the preceding section and should be used for introspection and discussion. Whenever possible, the questions are crafted to apply at a company, department, and individual level.

1. What is your brand's, departmental's, or individual's unique value proposition? How clearly does it express what makes you different? If you don't have a value

proposition, here is a quick tool to help you craft one. Simply fill in the blanks below:

For ________________ (core customer segment), who are dissatisfied with ________________ (current situation or customer pain) or who seek ________________ (something aspirational), my company/department or I offer ________________ (practical and emotional benefits), which will enable those customers to ________________ (lifestyle or business outcome).

2. To what degree is your value proposition known and understood by team members, current customers, and prospects?
3. What training areas might improve your ability to convert prospects or engage customers?
4. All sales decisions require a risk–reward analysis. What do prospects risk by choosing you? What rewards do they stand to gain? Conversely, what risks do your current customers face if they leave you? What might your current customers potentially gain if they leave your business and go to a competitor?

The magic isn't brotherhood – it's partnership

In a *Forbes* article titled, "The Pros and Cons of Sibling Partnerships," Amanda Neville identified the following risks of partnering with a sibling: "Family dynamics are uglier when they manifest outside of the family . . . Pressure is more intense when family is involved . . . Separating personal and business will be even harder than ever . . . Formalities tend to take a back seat."

When asked how they've navigated three decades of running a sibling-founded business, Aidan noted, "Up-bringing has a bearing on all relationships between business partners. David and I have longstanding trust and shared values around hard work and persistence." David adds:

> "It's like any pre-existing relationship – husband/wife, college roommates, etc. – where people choose to become business partners. Aidan and I get along well. We think the same way about many business issues and are complementary in other areas. For example, I understand customers well and envision solutions that meet their needs. In turn, Aidan brings those solutions to life through our products."

In addition to mutual respect, David (CEO) and Aidan (Head of Macquarie Government) suggest their leadership success results from carving out independent paths that fit their strengths. David uses a restaurant analogy to discuss the brothers' parallel but congruent leadership approach:

> "It's like Aidan is in the kitchen and I'm in the front serving customers. We communicate and work together to ensure our customers get what they want and need. However, most of our time is spent working independently, doing what each of

> us does best, having fun, and creating the greatest possible value. Our biggest challenges are making time to sit down together to ensure we are aligned and maintaining a relationship outside of work – a relationship that intentionally leaves work discussions behind."

David and Aidan's relationship offers each brother the freedom to work independently toward shared objectives and parallels an overarching management concept at Macquarie called "freedom within boundaries." That approach applies to all Macquarie leaders, managers, and frontline employees. Chapter 5 examines what "freedom within boundaries" means across the company and how you can apply it in your business and personal relationships.

Post-start-up growth – magic in transition

Having survived lean and mean start-up years in the mid-1990s, Macquarie became a publicly listed Australian Securities Exchange (ASX) company in 1999. David notes:

> "We were where many companies find themselves post-start-up: our growth created the challenges of a medium-sized business without the finances to meet them. Our decision to go public came from a need to raise capital. We had made solid profits but couldn't generate enough cash profit to fund the growth of our business. We used float proceeds from our public offering to build Australia's first data center. Self-funding was no longer possible, given the sizable capital outlay required for the

> project. Our options were either equity or debt, and we chose equity.
>
> "Being a public company also made it easier to secure bank loans when needed. Bankers know that there is more regulatory oversight on a publicly traded company, and it benefits the bank to have more people watching over a business."

Macquarie's ASX listing created a timely opportunity to expand into adjacent markets and accelerate its business rigor. According to David:

> "Unlike some companies who go public too early, we were reasonably prepared for the challenges and opportunities that came from being accountable to a large group of shareholders. As an owner, founder, and CEO, I suddenly had to dedicate about a third of my time to shareholders and others who offered input on our direction.
>
> "By going public, Macquarie became a better business. Our entire organization tuned in to managing risk and exploring opportunities. Knowing that we were accountable to 5000 shareholders kept us focused on being accountable for performance. Often, the challenge of a founder-led private company is that you mark your homework with too much self-empathy. Some private companies are driven by founders who obsess about revenue growth, others about profits.
>
> "A public company's discipline is that you must be accountable for sustainably delivering both. In a public company, shareholder empathy for

underperformance justifications is small. Solutions, consistent performance, and growth matter, and we've benefited tremendously from the value our board of directors provides."

Since becoming a public company in 1999, Macquarie's market value has steadily increased. The company's growth has been fueled by leadership's commitment to meet the needs of mid-sized and large business customers, intelligent investments in innovative offerings (Chapter 7 explores the impetus behind business growth in areas such as cloud computing in 2000 and cybersecurity in 2005), extraordinary customer retention (examined in Chapter 6), and cross-selling customers across product lines (addressed in Chapter 5). As Macquarie has expanded, David and Aidan have continued to face many other giants, some of whom – such as Verizon in government cybersecurity and Amazon in cloud services – targeted Australia from afar.

Magically defying gravity

Sean Aylmer, the host of the business podcast *Fear and Greed*, describes David Tudehope as "one of the longest-serving CEOs of an ASX-listed company." David's 30-year run as founder-CEO is particularly unusual in the rapidly evolving technology sector.

According to a 2021 *Harvard Business Review* article written by Bradley Hendricks, Travis Howell, and Christopher Bingham, the leadership requirements of a start-up bear little resemblance to "challenges such as streamlining operations, lowering costs, and managing an increasing number of employees, products, services, functions, geographies, and customers." This is only further complicated by the increased visibility and dispersed ownership of the CEO role post-initial public offering (IPO). Based on the authors' research, while companies with founder-CEOs enjoy an almost 10 percent higher company valuation at IPO, that value "essentially dwindles to zero approximately three years after firms go public," after which founder-CEOs actually detract from the value of their companies. However, the authors acknowledge that exceptions do exist.

David and Aidan are truly exceptions. They and the company's stable leadership team have steered the company from start-up to its present-day success by deploying a growth mindset, incessant curiosity, and untiring perseverance. As legendary basketball coach John Wooden said, "The best leaders are lifelong learners; they take measures to create organizations that foster and inspire learning throughout."

When asked how he continues to be relevant and a catalyst for Macquarie's growth, David said:

> "I've always sought mentorship and have worked with different coaches at various stages of my development. I read biographies to learn from people who create, build, and make a difference – people like Mustafa Kemal Atatürk, Turkey's founder and first President. His biography outlines how, in 15 years, he stewarded his country toward peace and prosperity by promoting education in rural regions and uncoupling religion and politics. It's inspiring to think of what leaders can do when they attack a transformational purpose."

David's curiosity, open mindset, and ability to integrate the ideas of others predate Macquarie. As a University of New South Wales student, David remembers sitting at a table in the university library and seeing an unshelved book about US President Calvin Coolidge.

According to David, "I opened it to a bookmarked page and found an insightful quote that I immediately photocopied. I kept that copy in my wallet, and it became very tattered as I referenced it in the early years of Macquarie'. The quote David later committed to memory goes as follows:

> "Nothing in this world can take the place of persistence. Talent will not: nothing is more common than unsuccessful men with talent. Genius will not: unrewarded genius is almost a proverb. Education will not: the world is full of educated derelicts. Persistence and determination alone are omnipotent."

Persistence is a critical part of Macquarie's magic. David notes:

> "Our success didn't follow the script of a Hollywood movie. We didn't devise a big idea and instantly moved from our garage into an office building. We just kept learning and persisted through tight times, growth spurts, economic downturns, pandemic lockdowns, and the uncertainties of a rapidly shifting industry. I've been fortunate to be surrounded by colleagues and team members who are persistent, determined, and passionate about working in our dynamic technology sector."

Practice your magic

1. In his book *The Speed of Trust*, Stephen M.R. Covey writes, "Trust impacts us 24/7, 365 days a year. It undergirds and affects the quality of every relationship . . . trust is not some soft, illusive quality that you either have or you don't; rather, trust is a pragmatic, tangible, actionable asset that you can create." How would you describe trust levels in your business or department?

2. What factors contribute to or degrade trust in your company or department? What "pragmatic and actionable" steps can be taken to increase trust? What actions will you need from others? What will they need from you?

3. How would you describe the developmental stage of your business/department (e.g., launch, rapid growth, slowed growth, maturity, or decline)? What skills have served your business/department well in the past? What skills are required for current and future needs?

4. In a *Harvard Business Review* article, Stanford Professor and "Growth mindset" researcher Carol Dweck wrote, "Individuals who believe their talents can be developed (through hard work, good strategies, and input from others) have a growth mindset. They tend to achieve more than those with a more fixed mindset (those who believe their talents are innate gifts)." Based on this description, to what degree do you and your colleagues demonstrate a growth mindset? Would you say your entire company operates from a growth mindset? Why or why not?

5. How do you ensure you continually learn (e.g., coaching, reading, attending conferences, or participating in dis-

cussion groups)? Where might you expand your growth and development opportunities (e.g., stretch assignments, mentorships, or shadowing)?

On a parallel journey

By reading this book and studying Macquarie, you are on a shared "growth mindset" path with David and Aidan.

I met David after he and his leadership team read my book *The New Gold Standard: 5 Leadership Principles for Creating a Legendary Customer Experience Courtesy of The Ritz-Carlton Hotel Company*. Subsequently, that book was distributed and discussed widely across Macquarie. Hopefully, you will do the same in your organization with *Customer Magic*.

In Chapter 6, you will see how ideas from industry experts led to process improvements that fuel Macquarie's world-class customer engagement. Also, in Chapter 7, you will learn how Macquarie's successful innovations came from systematically studying trendsetters through a process referred to as "international study trips."

Lest I get ahead of myself, let's wrap up this chapter with an insight David describes as "the most important lesson" he has learned at the helm of Macquarie. According to David:

> "All business success comes from taking care of people and enabling them to succeed. Care starts with your people and extends to all the lives they impact. By focusing on making a difference and providing service at the best price possible, I've been able to shift from running a start-up to building a business."

Sound advice.

Make your difference

- Take time to assess the gap between your prospective customers' expectations and what they are receiving from competitors.
- Language matters! Rather than use terms like "user" or "subscriber," talk about and treat your customers as people who deserve timely access to service professionals who will help them achieve individual or business success.
- Focus on prospects experiencing the most significant pain with their current product or service provider.
- While relationships are essential in business, buying decisions are typically made in favor of the provider who removes the most pain and creates the most significant value.
- Successful partnerships depend upon shared values, complementary skills, and actions that ensure mutual respect.
- The best leaders are lifelong learners, and they take measures to create organizations that foster and inspire learning.
- Pursue coaching and mentorship opportunities to increase your leadership and service skills.
- Read about and learn from people who inspire and transform the organizations and communities they serve.
- Success seldom follows a Hollywood script. There is no substitute for vision, effort, persistence, adaptivity, and a commitment to continual improvement.
- For sustained success in business and life, focus on caring for people and enabling them to succeed.

Chapter 3
From Purpose to Culture

"Any sufficiently advanced technology is indistinguishable from magic."
Arthur C. Clarke

This chapter is about company culture – a seemingly magnetic force that attracts or repels employees and customers. Culture is an invisible energy that either supercharges or impedes the growth of team members, customers, and businesses. More specifically, this chapter discusses Macquarie's company culture and what you can learn from it.

Culture, given its ethereal nature, is often misunderstood. Forbes Technology Council contributor Peter Messana suggests, "Culture is often conflated with activities and social functions, but culture is not built by having a ping pong table in the break room or by going out partying with the CEO."

To make culture accessible, let's work from a shared and easily understandable definition: *a company's culture is how people act at work*. By defining culture in the context of action, this chapter focuses on the tools and resources Macquarie dedicates to driving customer-centric behavior, accountability, and collaborative results.

Building the compass and guiding principles

Major League Baseball catcher Yogi Berra astutely observed, "If you don't know where you're going, you'll end up somewhere else." By developing a clear, concise, and actionable purpose statement – like the one created by Macquarie's founders – every person in an organization should understand their company's purpose and direct their actions accordingly. Co-founder and CEO David Tudehope shares the history and context behind Macquarie's purpose: "From the onset of our business three decades ago, Aidan and I wanted our purpose to be easily remembered so it would serve as a compass that guides action and decision-making." The result of that aspiration is Macquarie's purpose:

> To make a difference in markets that are underserved and overcharged.

Macquarie's 11-word purpose statement is memorable! Its concise and easily understandable language enables everyone at Macquarie to gauge their behavior relative to the desired outcome. For example, if an employee's actions aren't service-oriented or fail to deliver value, they should reverse course. Conversely, it's full steam ahead if their actions will serve others well or enhance value.

When I asked Paul Gedeon, the Operations Manager for Cloud Services, what the Macquarie purpose meant to him, he noted:

"Everything! The purpose represents customer service, technology, and people all brushed into one guiding concept. We must provide our customers with service and overall value they won't otherwise find in the market. I have grown up through different roles in Macquarie and see how important our purpose is to everyone here and how it plays out every day in what we do. I also know that living our purpose is a source of personal and professional pride for me and my colleagues."

In addition to articulating an empowering organizational purpose, Macquarie's leaders use restraint by limiting their values to four priorities. Uncluttered by long descriptions, Table 1 shows Macquarie's values.

Table 1: Macquarie's values

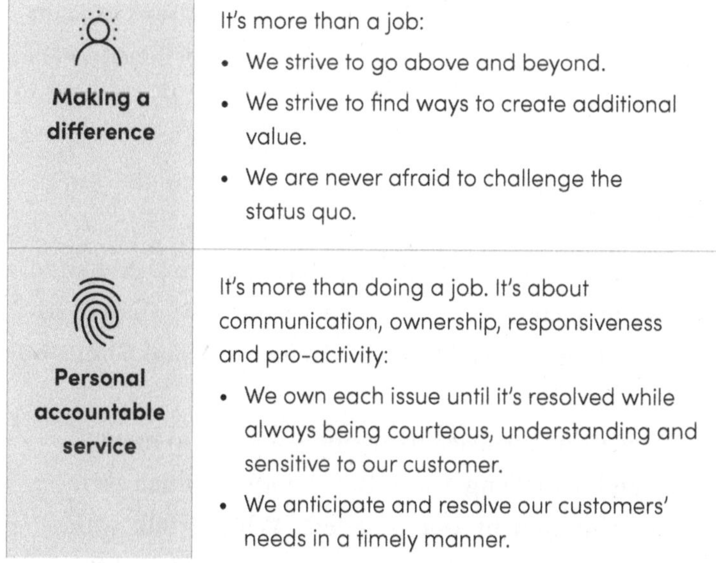

Making a difference	It's more than a job: • We strive to go above and beyond. • We strive to find ways to create additional value. • We are never afraid to challenge the status quo.
Personal accountable service	It's more than doing a job. It's about communication, ownership, responsiveness and pro-activity: • We own each issue until it's resolved while always being courteous, understanding and sensitive to our customer. • We anticipate and resolve our customers' needs in a timely manner.

	• We do not allow poor customer service, and we hold each other accountable to this promise.
Collaboration	Working together for success: • We cooperate across the business to ensure commitments are always met. • We make a point of understanding and respecting each other's roles. • We prioritise common goals over individual objectives.
Results	It's about making your numbers: • We celebrate achievements and congratulate others on their success. • We are adaptable and we persevere. • We focus on outcomes and solutions.

Later in the chapter, you will see how Macquarie captures stories that link values to the specific actions of team members. For now, let's briefly review each of Macquarie's four values.

Making a difference

Leaders at Macquarie emphasize that they are a mid-sized business that "punches above their weight." For Tony Pandher, Chief Operations Officer at Macquarie Cloud Services:

> "This value involves maintaining a start-up mentality and a challenger mindset – both of which were set in motion by our founders. When I talk with my team about making a difference, we discuss the

importance of believing that every person at Macquarie can and should positively impact others. We have the permission, power, and responsibility to create solutions and resolve issues for customers and each other."

Tony emphasizes that at Macquarie:

"Making a difference comes from being small enough to move quickly but large enough to have a sizable effect. Let's assume one of our engineers is working at a company the size of Microsoft, and they have an idea for product improvement. That idea would go through a lengthy approval process. If the idea somehow garners acceptance, it will still require countless iterations. That idea could be approved quickly at a small company but might not be implemented due to a lack of resources. Here at Macquarie, people make a difference and see that difference materialize. When team members suggest product changes, we huddle with the product team and get the key decision-makers in the room. Recommended changes are tested and launched so customers can enjoy swift, observable improvements."

Personal accountable service

Macquarie's value of personal accountable service (PAS) emphasizes the importance of owning a problem to its resolution. It is akin to a sign on the desk of US President Harry Truman that read, "The buck stops here." At Macquarie, team members can't hand off accountability. They are responsible for each customer they serve and should strive to understand the personal and professional impact of the customer's problem or need.

David Tudehope describes PAS this way:

> "The word 'personal' reflects genuine interest and connection with customers. Accountability from the customer's perspective means follow-through. If a customer shares that they are out of the office for a week, we demonstrate genuine interest by asking about their plans. Let's assume we learn that, unfortunately, they will be attending a family member's funeral. We empower and encourage our people to follow through with an appropriate gift, possibly sending flowers. Our customers are surprised and delighted by these acts of thoughtfulness."

You'll learn more about Macquarie's approach to gift-giving in Chapter 8. Later in this chapter, you will see how PAS is embraced across Macquarie and how it shapes behavior.

Collaboration

Macquarie's collaboration value complements PAS. While each individual is personally accountable for delivering service, the complexities of solving technical issues frequently require teamwork. This value functionally translates into "I will collaborate with others" and "I will seek collaboration from others." By asking for and accepting teamwork opportunities, Macquarie employees partner to make a difference for customers, thus providing collaborative value.

Sinead Murphy, a Service Delivery Manager in Cloud Services, explains that Macquarie's collaboration value applies to interactions internally and externally:

> "Clearly at Macquarie, my colleagues and I collaborate to assess and meet our customers' needs, but we also see our role as extending the customers' team. I demonstrate customer collaboration by listening attentively, building relationships, and managing projects. I know my customers, meet with them weekly through project launch, and stay with them – as does their personal customer technical officer – long after a project is complete."

Results

It's been said that people don't engage companies just to have someone be nice to them: brands that emphasize customer success and customer service must produce measurable business results. Those results fuel the brand's ability to serve more customers. Macquarie's results highlight the importance of assessing and learning from data. Chapter 5 will dive deeply into how Macquarie measures performance and service excellence.

Visionary leaders understand that values must translate into behavior that is salient to those they serve. David Dominguez, Director of Engineering at Adobe Marketo (the world's largest automation platform), told me:

> "Above all else, I want to work with reliable and responsive partners. With Macquarie, I also benefit from service professionals who take a personal

> interest in me, are quick to collaborate, and go above and beyond to meet our needs. I don't expect that extra personal attention, so it's been a pleasant surprise."

In short, Macquarie team members make a difference for customers like Adobe by working collaboratively to provide personally accountable service that drives results for both the customer and Macquarie.

Magic in simplicity and integrity

The presence of the Macquarie cultural framework isn't revolutionary. Most companies have a purpose statement and values. What is noteworthy, however, is the brevity and memorability of Macquarie's cultural infrastructure and the directional guidance these resources provide.

Well-crafted purpose statements and values paint a mental picture of a business's identity and purpose. They also show how the purpose can be achieved. Of course, we all know that words fall short when a company's purpose and values aren't reflected in decisions and actions across the organization. Put another way, actions speak louder than words.

Before Enron Corporation's scandal-plagued collapse in the late 1990s, leaders frequently discussed the company's four values: respect, integrity, communication, and excellence. Unfortunately for Enron's employees, customers, and shareholders, the actions of the leaders drowned out their words. Ironically, one of the company's values, integrity (which comes from the Latin word *integer* – meaning "whole" or "intact"), implies actions *will* match words. Someone should have explained that to Enron's leaders.

David Tudehope speaks to cultural integrity at Macquarie by noting:

> "One of the greatest tests of a company's purpose is whether leaders stay true to it when a purpose-centric decision comes with a cost. An example of this type of test occurred when we were set to launch a product that had garnered customer interest and pre-sales. From a commercial perspective, the product was good to go at the final gate or pre-launch check, but billing processes and operational procedures for handling service calls weren't fully in place. We had a choice: get the product to market, make budgeted sales, and work on billing and service issues post-launch, or delay the launch, lose sales, and have team members miss their KPIs. Our purpose clearly states that we exist to serve customers, so we postponed the launch and lost about half of the sales in the pipeline. When our product was released three months later, we knew it would live up to the service level implied by our purpose."

David's purpose-centric decision-making is in keeping with wisdom espoused by Horst Schulze, the founder of the modern-day Ritz-Carlton Hotel Company. In his book *Excellence Wins: A No-Nonsense Guide to Becoming the Best in a World of Compromise*, Horst notes, "Leaders sometimes complain, 'Oh, making decisions is so hard.' Most of the time, however, it's not – as long as the purpose of the organization is clearly stated. You set objectives that you know are good for all concerned, and then you force yourself to follow through in alignment with that vision."

You'll soon see how Macquarie leaders follow through by also spotlighting purpose-centric and values-based behavior through cultural storytelling and team-member recognition.

Practice your magic

1. Using the definition of culture is how people act at work, how would you describe your culture?

2. If your business doesn't have a purpose statement, take the time to draft one now.

3. If your business has a stated purpose and defined values, how memorable and succinct is that cultural framework?

a. Write down your company's purpose and values from memory. Did you accurately recall all of the elements?

b. Assume everyone in your department or company is asked to freely recall your cultural framework. What percentage of people would you expect to get it right? How can you help ensure everyone knows these cultural components?

4. On a scale from 1 to 10 (with 1 being "low" and 10 being "high"), how would you rate yourself, your department, and your organization on the ability to:

a. make a difference for colleagues

b. make a difference for customers

c. consistently provide PAS ("the buck stops here") to colleagues

d. consistently provide PAS to customers

e. seek collaboration from others

f. work collaboratively with others

g. drive measurable results for customers

h. drive measurable business results?

5. Think of a situation in which a person's words didn't match their actions. Without identifying the person, generally discuss the circumstances and impact of that mismatch.

Getting to the heart of behavior

Extraordinary service brands like The Ritz-Carlton Hotel Company and Macquarie seem to magically collect stories that show team members demonstrating value-based and purpose-centric behavior. To understand the secret behind this form of Macquarie magic, let's take a lesson from Penn Jillette (a magician in the famed Las Vegas-based duo Penn and Teller). According to Penn, "The only secret of magic is that I'm willing to work harder at it than you think it's worth."

At Macquarie, hard work is required to collect culture-affirming stories consistently. That work is done by six people called the "Heartbeat team." Aaron Tighe, a 23-year Macquarie veteran and State Manager for Macquarie Telecom, and Craig Lowe, a 25-year Macquarie leader and State Service Manager, oversee the Heartbeat program. Heartbeat team members collect, curate, and share "Heartbeat stories," highlighting Macquarie employees who take value-based and purpose-supporting action.

Aaron provides the evolution of Macquarie's customer storytelling efforts by noting:

> "Around 2007, we looked for a way to capture examples of behavior that aligned with the service component of our purpose. Our first attempt was called 'Customer Club.' where we asked customers if we could interview them after they told us they'd received excellent service. We cascaded those customer interviews throughout Macquarie and recognized the team members who provided the service."

David Tudehope adds:

> "Customer Club worked well initially as our employee reward focus generated considerable employee interest. However, after the first two years, we realized that we should recognize team members that did more than successfully deliver the expected and requested in a professional way."

With an unwavering commitment to catch and share as many positive stories as possible, Aaron and colleagues quickly transitioned from Customer Club to the Heartbeat program around 2011. Aaron continues:

> "Heartbeat is designed so employees can submit values-based, purpose-inspired stories of service. We have streamlined the program over its long run to make it easy for employees to offer their submissions. A short form appears when a team member clicks the Heartbeat logo on our intranet. That form reads,

> 'Who are you nominating, what's the customer's name, and please tell us the story.'"

Each week, the Heartbeat team meets to review submissions. According to Aaron:

> "We read every story as a group to see which ones have magic. We then pick out one or two stories that best reflect our purpose and values. Generally, we ask ourselves if this is an example of a person or team simply doing their job. If so, we will pass on the story. If it is more than standard service, we consider whether the story is an example of exceeding expectations or if it delivers 'wow.' For us, 'wow' transcends the 'exceeding expectations' category. 'Wow' stories involve team members leaving customers wondering, 'How did they think of that,' 'Where did that come from,' or, 'Where else other than Macquarie would I receive that kind of service?' 'Wow' has an emotional component. We also carefully select some 'exceeding expectations' and 'wow' stories that reflect simple service actions and others that involve more heroic effort."

According to Aaron, the Heartbeat team occasionally has to contact the person who submitted the story to get more details. That notwithstanding, the team consistently sends weekly emails to everyone at Macquarie. They also send a personalized recognition email to individuals involved in the selected stories and copy department executives into those acknowledgments.

Unlike companies that launch behavior-reinforcement programs with fanfare only to abandon them soon after,

Macquarie's Heartbeat team has sustained the program by enlisting managers to spark submissions when needed. David Tudehope notes, "While staff can nominate their own stories or their colleagues' service stories, we find managers are a particularly effective source of stories since, quite often, the staff who deliver the most amazing experience are very humble and take the most satisfaction from delighting the customer."

Fionán Mc Donnell, Macquarie New South Wales State Manager, agrees with David's assessment that managers must nudge service providers to get past their humility:

> "I used to feel uncomfortable talking about how I serve customers because it seemed like bragging. Since that feeling is common, I now onboard team members by letting them know the importance of sharing their service stories. That sharing enables us to learn from each other. Now I onboard team members with a story about a CIO who was considering Macquarie. She and I were meeting for lunch when I noticed she was a bit agitated. When I asked if she was OK, she told me she was missing her handbag and feared she had left it in a taxi en route to the restaurant. Upon contacting the cab company and determining they found her bag, she had difficulty giving the dispatcher the restaurant's location, so I asked if I could help. Upon ensuring the taxi driver knew where to go, I stepped out to receive her lovely Hermes bag and return it to her. I enjoy sharing this story because it demonstrates that service doesn't involve grand gestures."

Fionán told me:

> "As I read your book, *The New Gold Standard*, about The Ritz-Carlton Hotel Company, I latched on to the concept of having your 'antenna on and radar up' at all times, whether that is in a business lunch or when assessing a client's needs. I want team members to look for clients' unstated needs and share examples of how they uncover and meet them."

The Heartbeat team has sent weekly enterprise-wide emails for over a decade due to sustained oversight, untiring effort, and enterprise-wide collaboration. (Remember, collaboration is a Macquarie value.) Since Heartbeat's inception, countless employees have received personal and timely appreciation for living Macquarie's values and helping realize Macquarie's purpose. David adds, "Heartbeat is successful because its goal is clearly focused on capturing outstanding customer service stories to inspire other employees."

In addition to selecting stories every week, one or two of the most impactful Heartbeat stories are shared at Macquarie's monthly national videoconferences. Similarly, the best stories of each quarter receive extra recognition. Aaron adds:

> "At the end of the year, as part of Macquarie's broader recognition extravaganza – our version of the Oscars – we recognize the best service stories of the year in each of our divisions: Cloud, Data Centres, Telecom, Government. At that annual event, we award fun prizes and memorialize our best stories."

Can you imagine a better way to demonstrate what it means to make a difference, provide personal accountable service, collaborate, or drive results?

Practice your magic

1. Consider and share examples of customer service excellence you've provided or observed in your department or organization. Would you categorize your example as "standard," "above and beyond," or "wow"? What specific actions were taken by the service provider?
2. How are values-based or purpose-centric behaviors recognized in your department or company? How consistent and timely is that recognition?
3. When service behaviors are recognized, how frequently are those behaviors shared in the context of your company's purpose or values?
4. In addition to informal (naturally occurring) opportunities for sharing service stories, do you have a formal process (like the Heartbeat program) in place? If not, what would it take to launch one? How would you sustain that type of program?
5. What stands out about the Heartbeat program? What lessons can you take away from Macquarie's approach to collecting, sharing or recognizing team members' efforts?

The magic of storytelling

The National Geographic Society reminds us, "Storytelling is universal and is as ancient as humankind. Before there was writing, there was storytelling. It occurs in every culture and from every age. It exists (and existed) to entertain, to inform, and to promulgate cultural traditions and values."

Humans learn from written stories and oral traditions passed down for generations. Stories help us avoid pitfalls experienced by others and inspire us toward constructive action. More specifically, stories of service excellence evoke positive emotions. Those emotions, in turn, make each story memorable by activating stress-reducing hormones and neurotransmitters.

Aaron Tighe shares how these biochemical benefits play into Macquarie's commitment to untiring service storytelling:

> "Research shows that when people are served well, the person providing that service and the person receiving it experience increased oxytocin – a hormone linked to elevated mood. Surprisingly, research has also shown that people who witness those service acts get an oxytocin boost. Our goal at Macquarie is to have everyone engaged in service excellence. We want our organization to benefit from delivering, spotting, or hearing stories about making a difference through personal accountable service, collaboration, and being results-focused."

Improving corporate culture can sound like a daunting task or a project that company leaders and people in the HR department should drive. In truth, every person has an essential role in creating an outstanding service culture and an engaging workplace.

In *The Culture Playbook*, Daniel Coyle notes, "Culture is not a gift you receive; it's a skill you learn. And like any skill, it can be done well or poorly . . . What you might not know, however, is how much power you have to control, strengthen, and transform your group's culture – if you take the right actions."

Make your difference

- Arthur C. Clarke said, "Any sufficiently advanced technology is indistinguishable from magic."
- Simply defined, a company's culture is how people act at work.
- A clear, concise, and actionable purpose statement helps everyone in an organization know the company's purpose so they can behave accordingly.
- A company's purpose statement should be easily remembered and serve as a compass that guides action and decision-making.
- Well-crafted cultural concepts paint a mental picture of a business's purpose and what it takes to achieve it.
- Integrity (which comes from the Latin word integer, meaning "whole" or "intact") requires actions to match words.
- According to David Tudehope, "One of the greatest tests of a company's purpose is whether leaders stay true to it when a purpose-centric decision comes with a cost."
- Extraordinary service brands invest time and money to collect, curate, and share service stories. Through sustained effort, service storytelling is weaved into a company's culture rather than becoming an abandoned initiative.
- According to the National Geographic Society, "Storytelling is universal and is as ancient as humankind . . . It exists (and existed) to entertain, to inform, and to promulgate cultural traditions and values."
- You have the power to control, strengthen, and transform.

Chapter 4
It's Always About the People

"The magic formula that successful businesses have discovered is to treat customers like guests and employees like people."
Tom Peters

In 2004, I started working with the Starbucks leadership team. I later wrote two books – *The Starbucks Experience* and *Leading the Starbucks Way* – outlining how those leaders designed Starbucks's customer experience and sparked exponential business growth. In my early days with Starbucks, I asked then-CEO Howard Schultz a question I commonly pose to leaders and frontline team members: "What business are you in?"

Howard unexpectedly answered, "We aren't in the coffee business serving people. We are in the people business serving coffee." When I started working with David Tudehope at

Macquarie, I asked him that same question, and his answer was shocking. David said, "We are in the business of delivering amazing customer experiences. It just so happens we are also in the technology business."

Howard's answer was somewhat understandable, given that he was in the food service and hospitality sector, but how do you make sense of a technology CEO framing his business around customer experience? Aren't they supposed to be product-focused?

Over the years, I've come to understand the Macquarie story. I've seen how David and Aidan started the company with service as their differentiator (Chapter 2) and built a service culture grounded on a clear purpose, supportive values, and consistent storytelling (Chapter 3). I've also learned that Macquarie hasn't always had the right people in the right places to support the company's service aspirations.

In this chapter, you will learn about a time when Macquarie's hiring approach was less than magical and how leaders transformed the workforce by changing their approach to talent selection. Additionally, we will dig into Macquarie's robust talent development process and how that approach contributes to Macquarie's status as a world-class service provider and a Great Place to Work. As the chapter title says, you'll see how Macquarie's leaders build their business appreciating that it is always about the people.

When "better than the rest" isn't great

As you'll recall from Chapter 2, David Tudehope referred to Macquarie's purpose as a compass for decision-making. But what happens when that compass seems to point in two different directions – when service considerations pull towards one decision and cost savings pull towards another? David explains:

> "In our industry, everyone outsourced and offshored – meaning they've used third-party, out-of-country companies to run their contact centers. Those subcontractors were and continue to be located in countries where wages are considerably lower. By contrast, we've always provided support services from Australia, which has cost us up to three times as much per provider."

Around 2012, leaders at Macquarie decided to take a closer look at the costs and benefits of their call center staffing approach. As part of that evaluation, Macquarie brought in a consultant, and leaders toured the best contact centers in the US (more on innovation study tours in Chapter 7).

According to David:

> "That trip to the US caused us to reassess and view contact centers as a core business function for Macquarie as they are a crucial element of our customer experience – as opposed to a non-core, specialized and outsourceable function. We needed our contact centers to be staffed by Macquarie team members."

Macquarie's decision to provide Australia-based support services is recognized as a competitive advantage by customers such as Stephen Wells, Executive Director of Marketing, V3 Leisure (a leader in tourism exchange platform technology): "When stuff hits the fan, as it does in any technology business, we know we can call Macquarie at any hour and speak to someone based here, and they will help us. That gives me great comfort knowing we, and our customers, are in great hands."

A perceived customer advantage notwithstanding, Macquarie needed to justify in-house and onshore labor costs. To do so, Macquarie sought to offset labor expenses with savings derived from fixing customers' issues correctly the first time. Additionally, Macquarie had to look for leaders and frontline team members who could deliver elevated customer experiences and would act in the opposite way to the rest of the contact center industry. David said:

> "Despite winning recognition for our customer satisfaction levels around that time, we weren't content with being better than our competitors. To do this, we needed to throw out the call center industry's most common metrics of average hold time and utilization and replace them with customer experience as measured by NPS (Net Promoter Score™). The focus would move from cost management to customer experience."

Brought in to help elevate the customer experience at Macquarie's Cloud Service contact center – referred to as the Hosting Management Centre (HMC) – Naveen Gera, Head of Service Assurance, notes:

> "We had a different team in those days. They were all seasoned engineers who had worked elsewhere and developed patterns that weren't necessarily customer-centric. Back then, an engineer's daily responsibility might have been handling backup

tickets. If they had three backups and resolved them by 10 a.m., that engineer might consider their work done, even if other engineers were drowning in tickets. Despite our company's collaboration value, the staff on that team didn't demonstrate effective teamwork. To be responsive to the ever-evolving needs of HMC customers, we had to hire a different type of team member, update roles, and rewrite processes."

There's magic in creating a hiring profile

For HMC to be more service-oriented, COO Tony Pandher exercised broad discretion (more on Macquarie's "freedom within boundaries" empowerment approach in Chapter 5) and replaced existing HMC engineers. Tony explains:

> "I primarily recruited technology graduates from local universities so prospects wouldn't come to Macquarie with low service standards established during prior employment in the technology sector. Fortunately, I was supported by Macquarie's executive leadership team. However, David Tudehope, our CEO and co-founder, did ask me to explain the criteria I would use to select the right candidates."

Tony reports that he needed help articulating his hiring profile. Initially, Tony focused on qualities such as a candidate being in the top 10 percent of their graduating class. However, over time he was guided by two elements – Macquarie's brand essence and a framework best expressed by teamwork expert Patrick Lencioni. The brand essence component involved Tony looking for "enthusiastically human and technically literate" people. The Patrick Lencioni framework prioritized candidates who were intelligent and open-minded.

David Tudehope offers his perspective on seeking "enthusiastically human and technically literate" candidates:

> "We work hard to hire people who have a customer service gene – that is the 'enthusiastically human' component. We also want people with deep technical literacy, since we are a technology company. While it might sound easy to find this mix, our sector is filled with technically talented people who lack the enthusiastic human piece. Many are wonderful people who can be harsh with others who aren't technically up to their standards."

Finding the enthusiastically human and technically literate

When it comes to the importance of finding service professionals with enthusiasm, Norman Vincent Peale observed, "There is a real magic in enthusiasm. It spells the difference between mediocrity and accomplishment." To move the HMC from mediocrity, Naveen Gera offers examples of interview questions used to screen applicants:

> "We ask candidates to define what customer service means to them. We also ask them to provide examples of where they received outstanding and poor customer service. We are looking for a candidate's internal service standards. For instance, if a candidate offers an 'excellent service' story that sounds

more like 'standard service' at Macquarie, that candidate probably lacks the enthusiastic human gene. The same goes for people who can't describe elements of poor or excellent service at a level of detail or insight to suggest they will meet our expectations for making a difference through service."

Seeking team members who are humble, hungry, and smart

As you'll recall, Tony Pandher sought a clear and concise way to describe Macquarie's hiring profile to David Tudehope. Tony essentially sought people who had a great capacity for growth (hence Tony's interest in graduates who ranked in the top 10 percent of their class) and a desire to develop new skills and habits (as opposed to candidates who were content with habits they had acquired elsewhere).

Patrick Lencioni's book *The Ideal Team Player* gave Tony a model that succinctly expressed what Tony looked for in HMC prospects – people best described as "humble, hungry, and smart." Patrick explains that humble team members "lack excessive ego or concerns about status," are "quick to point out the contributions of others," and are slow to seek recognition for their own. They share credit, emphasize team over self, and "define success collectively rather than individually."

According to Patrick, hungry employees are always looking for more – more things to do, more to learn, more responsibility. Hungry people rarely have to be pushed by a manager to work harder because they are self-motivated and diligent. They are constantly "thinking about the next step and the next opportunity." Finally, Patrick suggests smart staff members are emotionally intelligent and have common sense about people. They tend to "know what is happening in a group situation and how to effectively deal with others . . . They have good judgment and intuition around the subtleties of group dynamics and the impact of their words or action."

With these humble, hungry, and smart dimensions in mind, Macquarie's leaders built an employee value proposition (EVP) to attract those candidates. That EVP distinguishes Macquarie from other employers by guaranteeing support for a new hire's future marketability.

Practice your magic

1. What business are you, your department, and your company in? Where do "people" and "service" fit into your answer?

2. How has talent selection accelerated or hampered you, your department or your company's purpose-directed success?

3. How do you define customer experience excellence? Do you gauge it against direct competitors, your sector, or the world's best service providers, irrespective of the industry?

4. What hiring profile do you, your department, or your company use?

5. To what degree does your department or business screen for people that are "enthusiastically human and technically literate," and "humble, hungry, and smart"? What would be gained if these criteria guided all staffing decisions?

The magic of an EVP

The first paragraph of a Macquarie document directed to engineering prospects titled "Employee Value Proposition" reads:

> "When you work for Macquarie Cloud Services (MCS), you are working for the best. Literally! We have been externally recognized as a Great Place to Work, have one of the highest employee engagement scores globally, and are regularly recognized as one of the best providers in the business.
>
> "This stuff doesn't just happen. It's because of our people, our employment strategy, and our investment in our workforce.
>
> "In operations, we look for the potential in people. We take great, innovative minds and help them to develop into what they can be. We know no individual's path is the same, so we've tailored many pathways and career opportunities to suit you. Whether you want to be an Engineer, a specialist, a Personal Customer Technical Officer, an architect, or a Service Delivery Manager – we have you covered. We will be with you every step of the way!"

Table 2 depicts Macquarie's EVP across five dimensions: culture, work life, organization, opportunity, and reward.

Table 2 – Macquarie's EVP

Culture	• Collaborate • Make a difference • Be personally accountable • Achieve results • Be engaged everyday • Be led by the best
Work life	• Agile working • Great work/life balance • City locations • The best equipment • Dynamic environment • Regular team events
Organisation	• A Great Place to Work • Industry recognised and awarded • Unmatched customer experience • World-class facilities • Most recommended provider • Publicly listed company
Opportunity	• A defined career path • A growth focus • Industry recognised certifications • Access to emerging technologies • Alignment of passion and job • Work with the experts
Reward	• Great compensation • Additional leave • Macquarie Club • Legends and MVP Program • Heartbeat • PAS gifts

Figure 1, a ten-year roadmap, shows how new hires can develop along their chosen career paths. It reflects how graduate engineers are hired to work in the HMC for two years and how Macquarie offers career pathways that extend ten years after the initial two-year contract.

Figure 1 – Example of Macquarie's ten-year development pathway

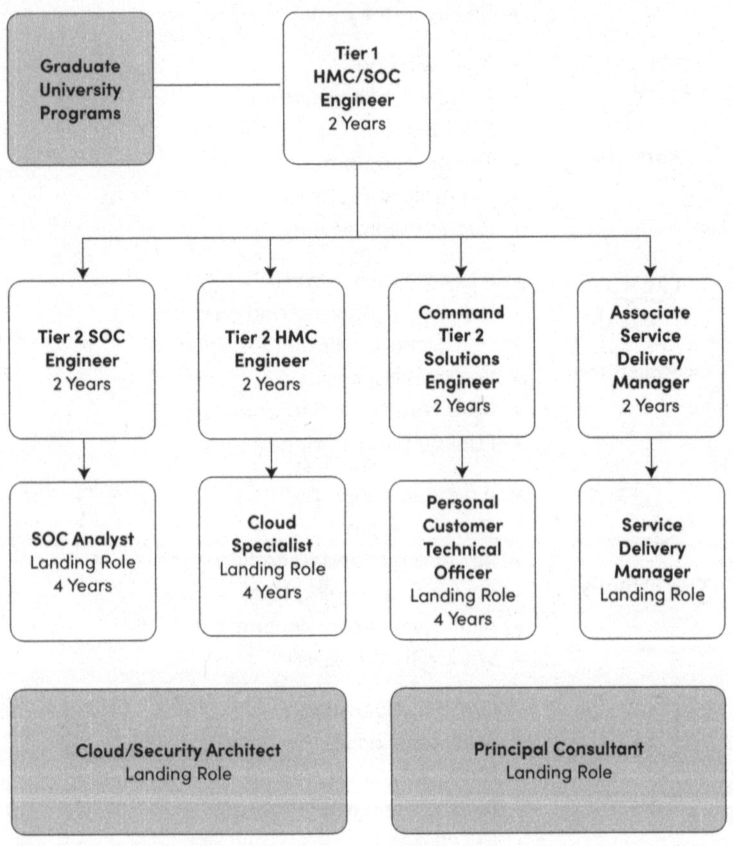

David explains the rationale behind telling a new hire that they will have their entry-level job for only two years:

> "It's important to be upfront with people and tell them that they will be making a commitment to

work in a demanding, 24/7 operation that guarantees and expects extraordinary technical skill development. If you meet all the expectations and achieve the predetermined learning objectives and externally recognized certifications, you will be poised for an exceptional technology career at Macquarie or elsewhere. You may also wish to take a break, travel, or pursue other interests at that two-year mark. If you stay with Macquarie after your two-year contract, we have established a ten-year program that supports a lifetime of technical learning. The power of this employee value proposition is that the two-year career sprints fit the commitment most new graduates are comfortable making and provided Macquarie-endorsed milestones where a graduate can plan to do something different."

Tier 2 Solutions Engineer Jake Osborne told me that he appreciated leadership's honesty about the challenges he would face in his first two years as an engineer. He was also grateful for Macquarie's commitment to his career development:

"Rather than soft-selling me, I remember being told that my university education was just the beginning of my career development and that if I hired onto Macquarie, the next two years would involve heavy-duty, hardcore development. That was absolutely true. Not only was I constantly learning and taking certification tests, but I was also working the night shift and commuting 90 minutes each way. As challenging as that phase was, I couldn't be more grateful. Here I am, four years into my employment, and there is no place I'd rather be. I am delighted with my growth path and savor the chance to work with my extraordinary and talented team."

Tony Pandher, COO of Cloud Services, adds:

"When I hire graduates, I assure them we put our commitments in writing. We pay for the certifications we require every six months. We increase their compensation as they gain each certification. David Tudehope and I will also be there every six months to celebrate their accomplishments publicly. Having been in this industry for a long time, I've seen tech companies get acquired and outstanding engineers struggle because they lacked industry certifications verifying their skills. We ensure our engineers get those certifications as part of their employment journey."

While *no* company can guarantee jobs for life, they can – as Macquarie does – guarantee investments in lifetime employability and long-term career paths.

Sharing knowledge and creating service innovation

In addition to growth that comes from on-the-job opportunities and certification courses, Macquarie's leaders expect engineers to share knowledge and collaborate on service innovations. As part of the transition to the HMC, Tony Pandher launched a knowledge-sharing program called "Top Gun." Tony explains:

"Early on, a new hire's knowledge acquisition depended upon who they sat next to. That led to inconsistencies and variable customer service. To fix that, we require everyone to publish articles in our knowledge management system and make creating and submitting those articles as easy as possible. Each article is reviewed and scored based on its complexity. Every quarter we celebrate and reward a Top Gun – the person who earns the most points from sharing their knowledge. We also use a heat-mapping tool to identify the most frequently referenced articles to identify training gaps. For example, one highly viewed article explained how to complete an expense report – so we turned that into a training topic."

Naveen Gera, Head of Service Assurance, adds:

"Top Gun is a tool to emphasize and reinforce the importance of everyone contributing to our shared knowledge database. The goals of this knowledge sharing are twofold – to ensure consistent service delivery and drive first-contact problem resolution. The consistency goal is like that of McDonald's – the company wants customers to have the same French fry experience in Melbourne and Miami. Similarly, at Macquarie, we want our customers to get the same accurate solutions every time from every engineer. As for first-contact resolution, accurate information enables frontline engineers to resolve nearly all problems without creating delay or escalation."

According to Naveen, an added benefit of Macquarie's knowledge-sharing database is how it "enables new engineers to see and improve on the work of those they aspire to become."

> "Imagine a senior engineer has authored an excellent article outlining the process for addressing a firewall issue. As a new engineer, let's assume you work those steps and identify one component that needs to be updated. You have real-time authority to change that process. Later, senior team members will review, validate, and celebrate your contributions. This approach helps all of us improve. It also shows our new team members the strengths of those who came before them and how they can immediately elevate the Macquarie customer experience. The process builds respect in both directions – senior engineers recognize new talent who contribute, and junior engineers appreciate the visibility from senior engineers."

From a frontline perspective, Dan Morgan, a Personal Customer Technical Officer at Macquarie, notes:

> "The Top Gun program created a framework for sharing articles and jump-started the thousand or so articles HMC team members have contributed. As a level-one engineer, I viewed Macquarie's approach to knowledge sharing as empowering because I could edit any article in the database. While all revisions are tracked, no article is locked away by an administrator. As such, I was entrusted to use my technical knowledge and commercial competency to create

> new articles or make necessary changes to existing ones. Somewhere along my tier-one journey, I realized those articles were there to help our existing team and serve future tier-one engineers. My contributions would ensure new hires weren't on struggle street when they arrived."

(Look for more on frontline empowerment in the next chapter.)

In addition to knowledge sharing, Tony reports that team members are expected to innovate service solutions consistently.

Tony shares:

> "As part of our teams' key performance indicators, engineers must deliver one piece of innovation every six months to help their team or help our customers. For example, our teams transferred information from one shift to another by having someone collect, integrate, and post relevant updates. As part of our innovation KPI, one of our teams recommended an automated alternative. When they proposed it, I asked if they needed my support and when they could complete it. Late that same day, they created a workable and lasting solution. Like all behavior we want to sustain, such as Top Gun knowledge sharing, we recognize and reward people for their service innovations. We've also found innovation breeds more innovation."

Practice your magic

1. What is your organization's EVP? How does it distinguish you from the competition?
2. What's your reaction to Macquarie leaders limiting entry-level engineers to a two-year contract? What benefits or risks are involved in that approach?
3. How clearly defined are career paths in your organization? How far do they project into the future? What can you, your department or your company do to enrich and extend career roadmaps?
4. What lessons can you take away from Macquarie's training and certification cadence and support?
5. How do you encourage or require knowledge sharing and service innovation in your department or organization?

The retention benefits of EVPs and career development

In 2014, Macquarie's approach to hiring university graduates for the HMC led to an article in *The Sydney Morning Herald* with the headline "Call center jobs . . . dead end or tech career stepping stone?'. Journalist Sylvia Pennington cited declining graduation rates among Australian technology programs and highlighted Macquarie's 75 percent staff retention rate, attributing it in part to the on-the-job experience and company-funded training Macquarie provided. She wrote:

> "Part-time University of Technology ICT student Finn Sheridan, 21, who joined Macquarie in 2013, is among those who have given it the thumbs up . . . 'University is very beneficial, but there's no experience like working. I can't tell you how much the experience has lifted me and given me so much knowledge.'"

Fast forward ten years and Finn Sheridan is still at Macquarie! This is largely thanks to Finn's diverse growth opportunities, which have enabled him to master technical and customer experience skills. Naveen Gera notes:

> "Finn started three weeks after I arrived, and he has grown with the business. Finn went from being a graduate engineer on my team to be one of Tony Pandher's senior engineers, offering consulting expertise to entry-level engineers and managing complex customer issues."

Finn is also an example of an "enthusiastically human and technically literate" team member who remains humble, hungry, and smart. Macquarie helped develop Finn, as evidenced by Finn consistently achieving "world-class" customer engagement scores that earned him special recognition at Macquarie. But I'll let Finn tell that story in Chapter 6.

For now, let's end this chapter as it started. Most if not all of us are in the "people" and "service" business. Accordingly, our success hinges on our ability to select and develop people who serve others well. With that talent selection and development in mind, here's your chance to review key takeaways.

Make your difference

- Labor costs are a factor in human service delivery decisions.
- Investments in service talent should produce higher first-time problem-resolution rates and improved levels of proactive service.
- For many businesses, customer contact centers are core business functions that make them challenging to outsource successfully.
- Effectively selecting service talent begins with a clear hiring profile.
- Successful service brands should screen for people who are enthusiastically human and proficient in their specific job functions.
- In the words of Norman Vincent Peale, "There is a real magic in enthusiasm. It spells the difference between mediocrity and accomplishment."
- Patrick Lencioni's model for the ideal team member focuses on individuals who are humble, hungry, and smart.
- Lencioni defines humble employees as being quick to point out the contributions of others and slow to seek recognition. They share credit, emphasize team over self, and define success collectively rather than individually.
- Hungry employees are described as always looking for more things to do and learn. They rarely have to be

pushed by a manager to work harder because they are self-motivated and diligent.

- Smart prospects and employees are emotionally intelligent and have common sense about people. They tend to know what happens in a group situation and how to deal effectively with others.
- An EVP should distinguish your workplace from competitors and appeal to prospects who fit your hiring profile.
- Look for ways to guarantee growth opportunities as a component of your EVP.
- Help prospects see how they will develop across a long-term career with your organisation.
- Focus on enhancing the future employability of your team, irrespective of whether employees choose to stay or leave.
- Consider incorporating knowledge transfer expectations and collaborative service innovation goals into your team members' performance plans.

Chapter 5
Seeking Freedom Within Boundaries

"Agree on the rules, unleash creativity, and watch the magic."
Howard Edson

Throughout the 1890s and early 1900s, Frederick W. Taylor – a self-proclaimed "consulting engineer in management" – significantly shaped leadership behavior. Taylor's system, Taylorism, analyzed every necessary and unnecessary human action involved in manufacturing. Taylorism required managers to do "time and motion studies" using stopwatches to drive machinelike efficiency. In short, the goal of Taylorism was to have managers achieve total staff conformity by affording team members *no* freedom to act beyond prescribed routines.

While work has changed considerably since the early 1900s (for example, shifting from a predominantly manufacturing to a service and information technology-based economy), traces of Taylorism remain. In his book *Drive: The Surprising Truth About What Motivates Us*, Daniel Pink shares four decades of research on human motivation in the context of organizational success. The overarching finding from Daniel Pink's comprehensive review is that current business models need to be upgraded based on three key elements: "1. *Autonomy* – the desire to direct our own lives. 2. *Mastery* – the urge to get better at something that matters. 3. *Purpose* – the yearning to do what we do in the service of something larger than ourselves."

Chapter 3 examined how Macquarie leaders bring the company's *purpose* to life by capturing and sharing purpose-directed and values-based examples. In this chapter, you will see how *autonomy* is maximized at Macquarie and how team members develop *mastery* in areas that matter most for sustained customer and business success. While this chapter emphasizes leader and manager decisions about organizational structure, everyone is responsible for fueling purpose, autonomy, and mastery at work.

"Freedom within boundaries"

About a decade ago, Macquarie's business plateaued. As a result, leaders took a multi-pronged approach to reclaim the company's entrepreneurial spirit. These leadership reinvigoration efforts included separating business units, streamlining organizational performance metrics, and decentralizing leadership and support functions.

David Hirst, Group Executive for Macquarie Data Centres, explains the business line uncoupling process:

> "Around 2011, our hosting and telecom product lines were unified. Telecom was our foundation and

hosting IT was our future. We positioned ourselves as a hosting-led telco. Unfortunately, the liabilities of that unified approach were highlighted when Amazon Cloud, a specialist in cloud services, entered our market. Unlike Amazon, we had telecom experts selling cloud services – *not* cloud specialists selling those products. Even though we were operating as a single business, we had two different core competencies – an IT core and a telecom core. So, we repositioned the company into two specialized business units based on those competencies. We further segmented our IT core into a commercial and a government business unit."

Before we explore how creating the Government business unit fueled autonomy and market growth for Macquarie, David Tudehope offers context for the decision to serve government clients:

> "In 2005, an Australian government agency asked us to help them. They struggled with a cybersecurity monopoly from a US-based multinational telecom conglomerate purchasing competitors. Given an absence of choice, that government agency reported annual rate increases and service reductions. Our prospective client advised us that they would recommend us to other federal government agencies if we did a good job for them. This opportunity fit perfectly with our purpose [to make a difference for markets that are underserved and overcharged], so we built a government-compliant cybersecurity offering. We continue working with the person who originally contacted us for government services."

Based on that client's recommendation and referrals from many other agencies, the landscape of Australian outsourced government cybersecurity has shifted dramatically. For example, Verizon's market share dropped from 100 percent of Australian government agencies outsourcing cybersecurity services to just 10 percent. By contrast, Macquarie went from 0 percent market share to 42 percent.

Aidan Tudehope, Macquarie's co-founder and Group Executive for Macquarie Government, links business unit specialization to that market growth:

> "Before we created our Government business unit, we were part of the commercial IT business. At that time, our enterprise sales teams engaged Australia's largest businesses, including government entities. While all large businesses have procurement and governance processes, we created a division of specialized Macquarie sales and service professionals. As such, we tailored solutions to meet government agencies' unique procurement processes, needs, and policies. When we launched the Government division, it was the smallest business unit we had ever created at Macquarie. I put my hand up to lead it because I saw what it could become."

Government is now the fastest-growing part of Macquarie's business and occupies a sizable and vital space for the company. Aidan describes his team as a "living and breathing government. We are free to hire extremely talented people who think similarly about governance and compliance issues uniquely valued in government settings."

Entrepreneurial spirit and empowerment

Many companies separate business lines but manage and support them in ways that constrain the autonomy of leaders in those businesses.

David shares:

> "Our freedom-within-boundaries approach is based on four key objectives. First, we wanted to keep alive the customer-centric mentality that Aidan and I have possessed since we founded Macquarie. Second, we wanted the leaders of each business unit to take an entrepreneurial approach to their respective businesses. Third, we inverted the normal empowerment model by providing full authority to business unit leaders except for explicit pre-set boundaries. Finally, we removed shared functions wherever possible and allowed each business unit to absorb them so their employees would drive their businesses' success."

Macquarie's empowerment of business units is evidenced by a central office comprising only four people – the CEO (David Tudehope), a Brand Manager, an Executive Assistant, and the CFO – with the minimum group functions. All other functions, such as recruitment, hiring, sales, marketing, product engineering, and service, are done at the business unit level. David explains:

> "From a political perspective, 'freedom within boundaries' is like having a small federal government that supports highly empowered state governments. The operational autonomy provided to our business

> units drives power and ownership back to the people in each business. In our freedom-within-boundaries model, the boundaries involve holding each business unit accountable to performance expectations, managing risk, and sound governance."

We've already explored Macquarie's "dynamic culture" in Chapters 3 and 4. Now let's look at the guidelines – or, as Macquarie leaders refer to them, "boundaries" – for decision-making and action. At Macquarie, those boundaries involve customer experience, revenue, and profitability metrics.

Winnowing it down to the vital few

Luke Clifton, Group Executive for Macquarie Telecom, has spent his career in telecommunications, including early employment at Telstra (more on that in Chapter 8). Luke, who has been with Macquarie for more than 15 years, reflects on a time when Macquarie's business performance metrics were overwhelming:

> "When I first got here, I was fascinated by how Macquarie maintained a start-up mentality. We were considerably smaller then and had mechanisms to ensure each leader knew what the others were doing. Since that level of sharing became unmanageable over time, we shifted to a balanced scorecard approach. During that phase, leaders would meet twice a year and discuss a long list of targets, objectives, timelines, details and KPIs. We sought to roll countless metrics into short- and long-term incentives and bonuses. Unfortunately, we didn't have unifying

> measures that rallied everyone, and balanced scorecard discussions were overly inclusive. For example, as much as I love my colleagues, I'm not an engineer and didn't need to know strategies to ensure their networks sustained 99.9 percent uptime. In essence, the metrics we reviewed and discussed were important to each of us individually but weren't necessarily essential for all of us collectively."

The flaws in Macquarie's balanced scorecard approach were especially evident during the company's performance plateau.

Luke shares:

> "During that time, we were only hitting about 50 percent of 250 performance indicators, but we were paying out approximately 83 percent of individual team member bonuses. Essentially, what we were measuring at the front line wasn't laddering up to success for Macquarie. As a result, our executive team engaged in robust discussions, which led to the three measures we've relied on to reignite our business."

Order to revenue to profit

The three aligned Macquarie performance metrics alluded to by Luke emerged from answering three fundamental questions:

1. How do we get a customer's order?
2. How do we turn an order into revenue?
3. How do we ensure our revenue is profitable?

Concerning the first question, Macquarie garners customer orders primarily by delivering a differentiated and elevated customer experience across all business units. Accordingly, Macquarie's leaders selected the Net Promoter System™ (NPS) to assess and enhance customer experiences. Chapter 6 is dedicated exclusively to Macquarie's use of the NPS and the system's derivative customer benefits. As a preview, leaders take a disciplined approach to customer experience management that distinguishes Macquarie through adherence to three steps outlined by Fred Reichheld, the creator of the NPS:

1. "categorizing customers into promoters, passives, and detractors through a simple survey"
2. "creating an easy-to-understand score based on that categorization"
3. "framing progress and success... thereby motivating everyone in the organization to take actions required to produce more promoters and fewer detractors."

As for the issue of assessing how orders turn into revenue, Luke Clifton explains:

> "Before we consolidated our metrics, we had many ways to measure revenue across the organization. For example, we rewarded salespeople based on gross margin. Other metrics included sales order revenue, customer loss, degradation, and yield decline. We were also filtering revenue by product, state, and geography. Because of these varied approaches and filters, we had difficulty rallying behind a single revenue metric that would make a difference."

Through considerable effort, Macquarie's leadership team landed on a unifying measurement index they called "net sales performance." It's calculated by taking sales order revenue minus customer loss minus yield decline at renewal. While this sounds complicated, Luke suggests net sales performance is readily understood across Macquarie: "It's actually a simple calculation, and we train it and talk about net sales performance consistently with everyone in our organization. Our people understand what revenue means at Macquarie, how we measure and track it, and what each of us can do to drive net sales performance."

That leaves us questioning how Macquarie ensures their "revenue is profitable." Not surprisingly, Macquarie's leaders use EBITDA (earnings before interest, taxes, depreciation, and amortization) as their profitability metric. However, Macquarie takes an unusual approach. Leaders train everyone in the organization on how to calculate EBITDA, why it's essential, and what each person can do to affect it. Luke notes:

> "We spend a lot of time conducting workshops and bringing people together to walk through and talk about generating a profit number from the EBITDA calculation. Most importantly, we help everyone have a line of sight to how they impact Macquarie's profitability. This definition of profitability is the easiest for everyone to understand and seek control over as it leaves out things team members can't control, like tax and accounting depreciation and interest on the company's loans."

Macquarie continually launches campaigns to ensure everyone understands how their behavior drives revenue and how revenue helps the business sustain and grow. According to Luke, "We want our people to understand NPS, net sales performance, and EBITDA from a Macquarie corporate, business unit, and personal level. Performance reviews also link to behaviors that drive these metrics."

Practice your magic

1. Are there residual elements of Taylorism present in your organization or department? If so, how is this freedom-limiting approach demonstrated? To what degree do these elements drive efficiency? If Taylorism is absent from your workplace, how does your organization balance individual freedom and process consistency?

2. How would you assess your department or business from team member autonomy, purpose, and mastery perspectives? What are your strengths and opportunities?

3. Would you describe your organizational structure as centralized (relying on top-down leadership and corporate support functions) or decentralized (dispersed decision-making and departmental independence)? What are the natural challenges that emerge from your structure? What are the benefits?

4. What measures does your department or organization use to answer these questions:

a. How do we get a customer's order?

b. How do we turn an order into revenue?

c. How do we ensure our revenue is profitable?

5. To what degree are your customer experience, revenue, and profitability metrics aligned, understood, and actionable across your organization?
6. How do you drive understanding for your metrics and cascade them into the performance plans of everyone in your business?

At Macquarie, freedom equals ownership

With customer experience, revenue, and profitability metrics in place, the leaders of each Macquarie business unit have the freedom to do what is necessary to drive business success. James Mystakidis, Group Executive for Macquarie Cloud Services, explains:

> "The Cloud Services business is *my* business. My team and I develop close relationships with our customers to help them succeed. In the process, we exceed our performance goals. My team lives our purpose and values thanks to our freedom-within-boundaries approach. We also make a tremendous difference for customers daily. Over the last eight years, our Cloud Services and Government businesses have contributed around $750 million in market cap value to Macquarie. Having the freedom to generate those results keeps me at Macquarie and gives me faith that we can easily double, triple, and quadruple Cloud Services' numbers."

James adds that the autonomy felt by business unit leaders also translates to empowerment at the manager and team member levels:

> "We measure employee engagement using the Gallup Q12, and each manager owns their team's engagement. There are zero corporate head office engagement activities, and I don't lead those functions for the frontline. What would a home office person or I know about driving engagement for a frontline team member? That team member, their manager, and colleagues are responsible for ensuring high engagement levels, customer service excellence, productivity, and profitability for everyone on their team."

David adds, "In keeping with our approach to measure customer experience, profitability, and productivity metrics, we selected the Gallup Q12 to measure employee engagement because it is easily understood and actionable at the frontline."

Gallup has researched human performance for over 75 years and validated 12 employee needs across more than 50 diverse industries. Those needs are summarized by the following statements:

1. I know what is expected of me at work.
2. I have the materials and equipment I need to do my work right.
3. At work, I have the opportunity to do what I do best every day.
4. In the last seven days, I have received recognition or praise for doing good work.
5. My supervisor, or someone at work, seems to care about me as a person.
6. There is someone at work who encourages my development.

7. At work, my opinions seem to count.
8. The mission or purpose of my company makes me feel my job is important.
9. My associates or fellow employees are committed to doing quality work.
10. I have a best friend at work.
11. In the last six months, someone at work has talked to me about my progress.
12. This last year, I have had opportunities at work to learn and grow.

By choosing an accessible and useful tool, Macquarie's employee engagement success is quantitatively reflected in an extraordinary Q12 completion rate of 99 percent and an exceptional aggregated engagement score of 4.24 on a five-point scale.

Bill Gaw, Client Director Strategic Accounts for Macquarie Telecom, offers a tangible example of the process Macquarie deploys to achieve qualitative employee engagement success:

> "The Q12 process provokes honest and at times contentious discussions. In the Telecom business unit, for example, Q12 results suggested that people felt our rewards and recognition structure favored salespeople. Specifically, we have an incentive program called '100% Club,' where salespeople who hit 100 percent of their sales target go on two trips a year anywhere in Australia. There wasn't a parallel

program for engineers, those who deliver projects, or people who handle escalations. Based on feedback, we developed an engineers' club to recognize and provide a learning experience for them. This is just one example of how we are encouraged to speak out and take responsibility for improving our peer-to-peer culture."

Separate business units all moving in the same direction

An inherent risk in a highly decentralized model is business units operating so independently that they fail to benefit from synergies and cross-sale opportunities. To combat that risk, David Hirst, Group Executive, notes:

> "We ground ourselves to our common purpose and shared values. While I run my business unit, I am also looking to cross-pollinate other Macquarie product lines. Each business has different product sets, marketing teams, and engineers, but we intersect around prospect and customer needs. For example, a customer might contact Macquarie for business telephone service. As the Telecom team learns about their customers' business, they might identify underlying needs for our Cloud or Data Centre business solutions. We are always on the lookout for how we can collaborate for the benefit of our customers and the success of all Macquarie business units."

David Tudehope adds:

> "When we initiated our freedom-within-boundaries approach, we had concerns that the structure would limit cross-selling between business units. On the contrary, we've increased sales between most businesses because cross-selling is driven by customer intimacy. When leaders and frontline team members hold themselves accountable for customer success, they get to know their customers and offer all relevant Macquarie solutions. Across the Executive team, we've also worked to ensure there are no disincentives for frontline teams or managers to present the products of other business units. Everyone receives equal credit for sales within and across business units."

Leaders have developed a language to guide discussions and decision-making that enables Macquarie's business units to work interdependently. James Mystakidis explains:

> "Group Executives sometimes wear a business unit hat. Other times we need to remove that hat and replace it with one that focuses on the needs of the enterprise. We've simplified terminology from our balanced scorecard methodology to signal these different situations. That terminology involves *level zero* versus *level one* conversations. We call anything related to the company or enterprise a 'level zero' conversation. Anything connected to business units is referred to as 'level one.' This language helps frame our business unit and enterprise conversations. A level one conversation is about what my team and I will do to make Macquarie Cloud Services the world's best. I'm competing at a global level, and I'm

driving the best possible Net Promoter Scores, net revenue, and EBITDA. As our business units achieve level-one goals, we collectively drive level-zero profits and shareholder value."

David Hirst adds:

"Usually, it's easy for us as an executive team to look at level-zero leadership opportunities and make decisions that produce the best result for Macquarie over the long term, setting aside the short-term interests of our respective businesses."

Practice your magic

1. Using Gallup Q12 categorizations, fully engaged team members can be considered "owners." somewhat engaged staff can be viewed as "renters" and disengaged team members can be considered "squatters." How would you describe the ratio of owners to renters to squatters in your department or business?
2. What factors contribute to colleagues taking or deferring ownership of customer experience, revenue or profits in your business?
3. What data shows your organization's level of empowerment or ownership (e.g., engagement survey results, productivity metrics)?
4. How do you distinguish departmental or business unit needs from transcendent enterprise-wide needs (e.g., level zero and level one discussions)?

5. How effectively do individuals and departments work together to overcome siloed thinking to address broader customer and business objectives?

6. How does your department or organization seek to build bridges between business units?

Creating mechanisms for ownerships

Before we close this discussion of "freedom within boundaries," let's look at a process called "Not on My Watch" (NOMW) that Macquarie's leaders use to maximize frontline ownership behavior and achieve empowered solutions. Aaron Tighe, Western Australia State Manager, explains:

> "Not on My Watch 'is a weekly forum where everyone in the company is encouraged to share observations related to product or customer issues. These meetings empower all of us to observe and participate in problem resolution. At a NOMW forum, for example, Account and Service Managers (those directly responsible for local customer relationships) raised a concern that some of our customers were experiencing unacceptable broadband disruptions, which resulted from a lack of resilience and redundancy in the network of an underlying carrier. With Operations, Network, Service Assurance, and Sales teams and leaders in attendance, our COO, Steve Peck, took immediate ownership of the issue and asked our Head of Engineering and Carrier Manager to investigate, understand, and find a resolution. Weekly Friday

updates were provided to forum participants. Following discussions with the underlying carrier, additional redundancy was confirmed, guaranteed, and built into the network over the next few months. This service enhancement was managed and tested by the Macquarie Engineering Group. Thanks to joint ownership taken across business units, we partnered with the underlying carrier to swiftly remediate the outages and fix underlying issues that affected some of our customers."

Aaron shared another example of the benefits of the NOMW forums, noting:

"Customer-facing service delivery managers picked up occasions where customers' bills were increasing suddenly during the month. This created customer issues, internal inefficiencies, and unnecessary billing disputes and credits. As the Service Managers investigated the bill details, they had insights into what might be contributing to the surges. At the forum where the Service Managers raised the issue, a leader was designated to own the problem's resolution. By the following week, the root cause was confirmed and, through the coordinated effort of the IT, Engineering, and Service Assurance teams, the problem was permanently fixed. In a matter of weeks, a single Service Delivery Manager activated the NOMW forum to bring together teams from across business units to investigate and ultimately resolve an important customer issue with haste."

Everyone at Macquarie is responsible for ensuring customers' concerns don't remain "on their watch." The extraordinary results generated through NOMW come from bringing decision-makers together to swiftly solve customer issues using a cross-business approach. Macquarie has developed a parallel forum to raise and resolve issues related to inefficiencies that waste time and negatively impact the employee or customer experience. That workforce empowerment process is called "Not on My Time" (NOMT).

Workforce engagement and empowerment have become interchangeable and distorted business buzzwords. In a *Huffington Post* article titled "How Empowering Your Employees Helps Improve Business," Natalie Lambert describes employee engagement as the "holy grail" of the modern workplace, something everybody wants to get right but few know how to achieve. She says that despite 70 percent of executives being aware of the importance of engagement, many leaders don't understand how engagement differs from empowerment and how the former depends on the latter. Employees can be engaged without being empowered, but "these employees face a higher likelihood of frustration, burnout, disengagement, low productivity, and attrition." When engagement stems from feeling empowered at work, however, "These employees are 67 percent more willing to put in extra effort on the job. They're also more willing to innovate and take the creative risks that help drive business growth and revenue gains."

Leaders at Macquarie understand that employee empowerment drives engagement. They also understand how empowerment fuels employee autonomy, mastery, and ownership behavior. Macquarie's "freedom within boundaries" approach drives empowerment, employee engagement, customer success, and Macquarie's growth.

Before we explore Macquarie's approach to customer engagement, here are a few chapter takeaways.

Make your difference

- At the turn of the 20th century, the management approach called "Taylorism" encouraged managers to drive total staff conformity, with team members having no freedom to act beyond prescribed routines.
- Despite changing economic factors, traces of Taylorism remain in many businesses.
- In his book *Drive*, Daniel Pink summarizes three decades of scientific research on employee motivation and highlights three drivers: autonomy, mastery, and purpose.
- To maximize autonomy, mastery, and purpose, companies may need to make changes that include developing specialized business units and creating clear guidelines and metrics.
- Business leaders may also need to consider a growing trend toward decentralized business operations.
- Assuming business units are allowed to operate with autonomy, they should be yoked together by performance metrics that address questions like the following:
  - How do we get a customer's order?
  - How do we turn an order into revenue?
  - How do we ensure our revenue is profitable?
- Businesses that foster high levels of autonomy and mastery invest in helping everyone in their organization understand how they contribute to measurable customer success, revenue generation, and profitability.

- Natalie Lambert describes employee engagement as the "holy grail" of the modern workplace.
- Employee engagement depends on employee empowerment.
- Companies that strategically and tactically drive employee empowerment enjoy increased discretionary effort from employees, more productivity, and substantially increased revenue.

Chapter 6

The Art and Science of World-class Customer Experience Delivery

"Customer magic happens when team members listen, learn, design, and tailor experiences."
Tony Hsieh

Early in my career, I had to make a case for investing in continuous customer experience improvements.

Some 34 years and 12 books later, leaders clearly understand that customer experiences create brand differentiation, repeat business, and positive word-of-mouth. A study by Gartner shows that from 2010 to 2018, the percentage of business executives who report that they compete *primarily* on customer experience jumped from 36 to 68 percent – with 81 percent of leaders expecting that in the near future, they would be competing largely based on the customer experiences they provide.

Despite the accepted importance of customer experiences, many companies struggle to create memorable and engaging interactions, let alone maintain them. As a customer experience consultant, I often see companies undertake countless customer experience initiatives that fail to increase customer engagement or drive business growth.

Despite strategic prioritization and concerted effort, the 2022 American Customer Satisfaction Index (ACSI) showed that customer satisfaction had hit a 17-year low (see Figure 2), and satisfaction is a low bar compared to the relationship criteria Macquarie measures – customer *engagement*.

Figure 2: The American Customer Satisfaction Index (ACSI)

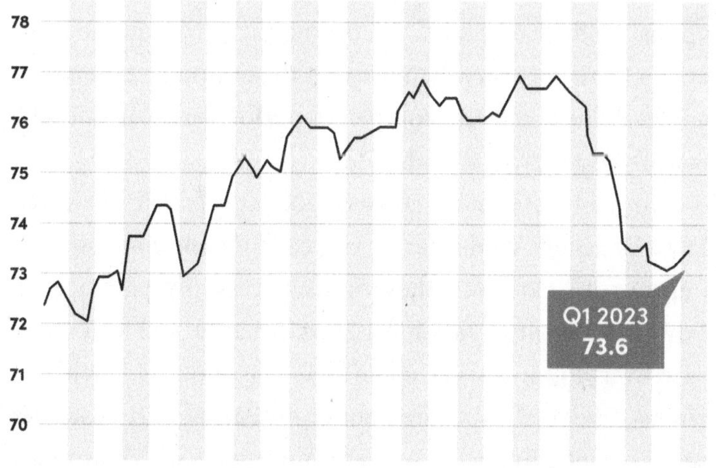

This chapter explores how Macquarie creates a consistent, world-class customer experience. We will first examine

Macquarie's selection and use of a customer engagement system and then review Macquarie's processes for incentivizing, rewarding, and sustaining outstanding experience delivery. Finally, we will link Macquarie's customer-related achievements to key performance indicators and review a story of customer service excellence.

Success begins with measurement

As you learned in Chapter 2, Macquarie's co-founders, David and Aidan Tudehope, built their company on a service experience value proposition that starkly contrasted with legacy telecom providers. Throughout Macquarie's early history, the company grew by living up to and exceeding its service promise and fulfilling its purpose. However, in David's words, leadership wasn't content to be "the best of a bad lot in telecom and tech. Instead, we decided to do the opposite of the industry." Accordingly, the Macquarie leadership team consistently improved the customer experience and benchmarked the company's performance against the world's best service brands.

To achieve David's goals, Macquarie leaders followed Peter Drucker's guidance: "If you can't measure it, you can't improve it." However, they didn't necessarily embrace W. Edwards Deming's wisdom: "Just because you can measure everything doesn't mean that you should." David explains, "We've always cared about measuring our customer service. Unfortunately, we were misguided with too many early measurements and strategies that resulted in limited improvements."

David is referencing a time when Macquarie was more of a top-down organization, with centralized Human Resources and Marketing departments. James Mystakidis, Group Executive, picks up the story from there:

> "We were on a customer satisfaction (CSAT) journey at the time, led by someone on the marketing team who oversaw a roughly 50-question customer survey. Given the survey's length, it took customers a long time to complete it."

The cumbersome nature of those surveys also led to low response rates and companies having a less-tenured team member complete them. James continues:

> "As an executive team, we would meet for half a day to review a 200-slide deck summarizing survey results, including roughly 20 recommendations to improve customer satisfaction. We'd look for progress on the recommendations from the prior semi-annual survey but wouldn't see our efforts having much effect on satisfaction levels."

David describes the shift away from Macquarie's lengthy customer satisfaction survey process, noting:

> "It was clear that we had too many questions and that our measurement process wasn't helping us improve. Looking for a better solution, I read a *Harvard Business Review* article by Fred Reichheld titled 'The One Number You Need to Grow.' It captured our situation perfectly."

In that article, Fred Reichheld wrote about the issues

with most customer satisfaction surveys, saying, "They tend to be long and complicated, yielding low response rates and ambiguous implications." He also described them as "rarely challenged or audited because most senior executives, board members, and investors don't take them very seriously" because of the weak correlation between their results and profits or growth.

In that same article, Fred shared the results of two years of research he and colleagues conducted through the consulting group Bain & Company. The unexpected breakthrough from that field research was the finding that a single question was highly correlated with business growth. That question, referred to as the Net Promoter Score™ (NPS), read:

> "How likely is it that you would recommend [company X] to a friend or colleague?"

The response options to the question ranged from 0 to 10, with 0 being *not* "likely to recommend" and 10 being extremely likely to recommend. Survey respondents were categorized into three groups: those who selected a number from 0 to 6 were labeled "detractors," 7s and 8s were "passives," and 9s and 10s were "promoters." The NPS was calculated by subtracting the percentage of detractors from the percentage of promoters, leaving a possible range from −100 (100 percent detractors and 0 percent promoters) to +100 (0 percent detractors and 100 percent promoters). The distribution of scores tended to follow a bell curve, with most scores registered around 0 (see Figure 3).

Figure 3: The NPS distribution range

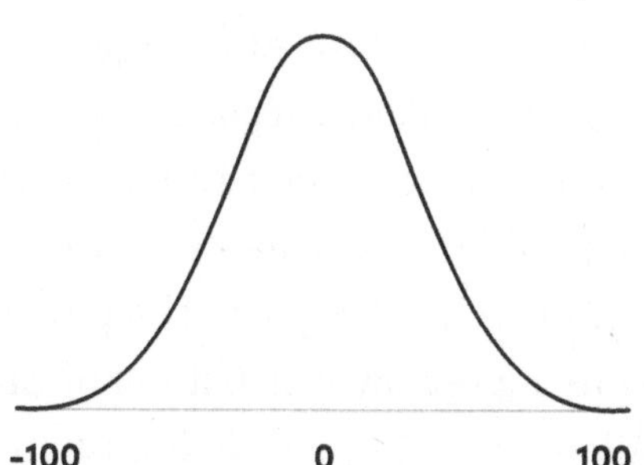

After this research, Fred Reichheld wrote *The Ultimate Question* and collaborated with Rob Markey on a book titled *The Ultimate Question 2.0*. Those works suggest slightly streamlined wording for the question – it's now typically presented as "How likely *are you* to recommend [company x] to a friend or colleague?" Leveraging emerging research, Reichheld and Markey outlined the processes companies should follow to use "likely to recommend" responses as a catalyst for business growth. Those processes broaden the concept of NPS from Net Promoter Score to Net Promoter System.

Given this context, David picks up the story of Macquarie's use of the NPS:

> "After reading Fred Reichheld's initial article, I was pleased to have a way to quickly measure our customers' experience and leverage that input to make timely improvements. I also saw NPS as a way to rally our organization around a single metric that could predict growth and enable us to benchmark ourselves against other service leaders.

"Unfortunately, one of my biggest regrets in business happened after I recommended the NPS question to our team. Instead of arguing that the single NPS question should replace our lengthy satisfaction questionnaire, I agreed to allow our marketing team to add the NPS question to our existing 50-question survey. In the spirit of empowerment, I didn't want to impose my will, but in hindsight, our failure to adopt the NPS as our only customer experience question took us two years to remedy, slowed customer experience progress, and limited our ability to benchmark ourselves with others."

David adds:

"A couple of years later, I was invited to a breakfast presentation by Rob Markey, the co-author of *The Ultimate Question 2.0*, and I came back the convert and overrode the strong objections of the marketing team to end the 51-question customer survey and replace it with the ultimate question. I realized that this change was essential for us to measure how well we were realizing our purpose. I also appreciated that the marketing team enjoyed the challenge of analyzing our complex survey responses and being at the center of customer experience conversations. However, we needed to simplify customer experience measurement and shift the NPS survey process and analysis to operations leaders. These leaders, in turn, embedded NPS into their processes, embraced the power of simplicity, and demonstrated the greatest ability to effect change."

Since then, Macquarie has refined its use of the NPS. For example, commensurate with driving empowerment and ownership (see Chapter 5 – Freedom Within Boundaries), the Macquarie corporate office doesn't attempt to be the catalyst for NPS's success. Instead, each business unit oversees the deployment of its NPS.

Macquarie's commitment to the NPS process

Across business units, Macquarie takes a rigorous approach to collecting and deploying customer input. Naveen Gera, Head of Service Assurance, stewards the NPS for Macquarie Cloud Services and trains Macquarie customers to use NPS effectively in their businesses. (More on this customer training in Chapter 8.)

Naveen provides an overview of Macquarie's NPS process by noting:

> "We ask the net promoter question across multiple corridors – or phases – in our customer's journey. We name those phases from the customer's vantage point. Specifically, we assess our customers as they contract with us, receive products or services, pay for what they receive, use services, and recontract.
>
> "Across corridors, we seek customer input on the quality of completed transactions (NPS-T) as well as the strength of our relationships (NPS-R) with the individual that owns our contract with the customer. We ask for NPS-T feedback after each completed transaction and seek NPS-R feedback at six-month intervals during a customer's contract."

Figure 4: Corridor segments

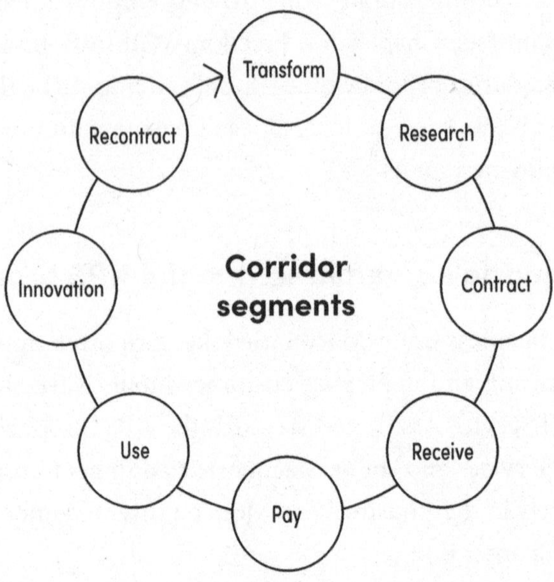

Transactional NPS surveys are initially triggered by an event such as contract signing ("contract"), fulfilling an order ("receive"), or completing an inbound service request ("use"). In the "use" example, a Macquarie team member will end the interaction by asking the customer to take a short survey via interactive voice response (IVR). This automated telephone system integrates prerecorded messages and text-to-speech technology.

NPS-R input is solicited by a Macquarie employee who sits outside of all business lines. Every six months, this team member reaches out to the customer's senior manager – usually a Chief Financial Officer or Chief Information Officer. After a response to the net promoter question is secured during the relationship call, the Macquarie team member asks brief follow-up questions that explain the score's rationale and what, if anything, could be done to improve the customer's service relationship with Macquarie.

Unlike many companies for whom I've consulted, Macquarie's process is consistent, efficient, and inclusive. It minimizes sources of bias and produces a remarkable response rate approximating half of all transactions. That high sample rate drives robust and reliable transactional and relational insights across contact points and throughout the customer's brand journey. Macquarie also receives input from stakeholders across varied functions in their customers' organizations. For example, NPS-R surveys generate feedback from senior decision-makers, and "use" surveys gather input from those needing issue resolution.

Throughout the writing of this book, I discussed Macquarie's NPS strategy with Fred Reichheld, the creator of the NPS. Specific to questions about the role leaders play in driving NPS success, Fred shared:

> "The foundational element for a successful Net Promoter System is a leadership team that embraces the central philosophy behind NPS – that the only way to grow a prosperous business is to inspire team members to treat customers so they come back for more and refer their friends. They view the organization's primary purpose as enriching their customers' lives. So corporate strategy, feedback, recognition, and rewards for employees are geared toward achieving this purpose."

From collecting to effectively using customer input

Customer experience professional Bruce Temkin advises, "Don't waste customers' time asking them questions unless you are prepared to act on what they say." At Macquarie, customer feedback is a catalyst for unwavering, real-time action. When the IVR captures an NPS-T response, the service provider and their supervisor receive an email citing the customer's input. The NPS refers to this type of employee-directed communication as "closing the inner loop."

Naveen expands on what happens after the supervisor/service provider email is sent:

> "When we get a detractor (a 0 to 6 score out of 10) or a passive (a score of 7 or 8 out of 10), the supervisor of that particular engineer or customer agent must follow up with the customer within 24 hours. The supervisor kindly and respectfully asks the customer what led to the score, how we can address any lingering issues, and what we can do better going forward. Since customer calls are recorded to ensure service quality, we listen to the call and look for any breakdowns. For example, a customer might have a billing inquiry that wasn't completely resolved. We then devise a recovery plan that incorporates the customer's feedback at follow-up. That plan might involve changing something on the customer's bill or coaching a team member to address the issue differently. If a high-priority item gets missed, we use the breakdown as a training opportunity for the entire team."

In the NPS, using customer feedback to engage customers directly is called "closing the outer loop."

Macquarie's process for activating relational input from the NPS-R is similar to that of the transactional NPS. The net promoter response is captured during the outbound call and entered into Macquarie's customer management database. The score and subjective feedback from the call are sent to Regional Managers. Aaron Tighe, Regional Manager for Western Australia, explains:

> "When a result is passed through as a detractor, or a passive, we call the customer within 24 hours. Our purpose is the same as in the transactional follow-up call. We want to demonstrate our concern, listen for reasons they weren't delighted, and see what we can do to improve their experience. We stay accountable to the customer's feedback and remain in touch with the customer until the issue is resolved. Customers appreciate our calls and are surprised to receive personal follow-up from a telecom/technology company."

In addition to closing the feedback loops and resolving issues with customers categorized as detractors and passives, leaders intermittently contact *promoters* to thank them for their response, letting them know their input was reviewed and that their business is appreciated.

Going from active to proactive

Not only does Macquarie take follow-up action, but leaders also routinely use that follow-up feedback to anticipate other customer needs and build innovative solutions. Naveen Gera provides an example of these far-reaching and proactive actions, noting:

> "We send monthly reports to our customers, giving them a full view of their services and how they performed that month. During an NPS follow-up call, one customer shared that our monthly feedback wasn't sufficient. From a compliance perspective, they needed daily reports to verify that their nightly backups were successful. In response to their concern, we spoke to our engineers in the HMC. They wrote a script for the customer to receive a daily email showing green (the backup was successful) or red (the backup was unsuccessful). We shared this solution with our product team, and now it's a service option for clients with similar needs. We have many other examples where a solution crafted in response to NPS follow-up is applied proactively to prevent that issue from surfacing for other customers."

Naveen's daily reporting example, and others like it, are presented at Macquarie NPS workshops. These workshops bring together team members from all business lines. (As discussed in Chapter 5, this is an example of how Macquarie creates connections between business units.) During these biannual workshops, each business unit shares challenges, breakthroughs, opportunities, and best practices for using NPS data to improve customer experience and organizational success.

In discussing Macquarie's proactive use of the NPS with Fred Reichheld, he responded:

"Most good innovation comes from the frontline employees and supervisors since they have the deepest understanding of customer problems and how they could be solved. The Net Promoter discipline of closing the loop with every detractor – along with a sampling of passives and promoters – stimulates the learning and innovation process."

Practice your magic

1. Would you agree that your department or business competes primarily based on customer experience? If so, why? If not, what is your competitive battleground?

2. How do you assess the quality of customer transactions and the strength of your customer relationships?

3. Discuss the degree to which your customer experience assessment and improvement processes:
   a. yield high response rates,
   b. assess all phases of the customer journey,
   c. identify customers who require follow-up discussions,
   d. close internal and external feedback loops,
   e. resolve issues and generate proactive solutions.

4. How do you share best practices for turning customer input into customer experience solutions across your department or organization?

5. Discuss examples of when customer listening led to process innovation or product breakthroughs.

The magic of transparency

We've seen how Macquarie leaders follow up with customers based on responses to the net promoter question. Now let's look at how those customer responses shape frontline behavior. As you'll recall, team members receive an email after a customer rates a transaction. That rating is also posted on monitors across Macquarie showing aggregate NPS performance by each department and for individual team members. This data is refreshed in real-time.

David Tudehope explains how Macquarie's approach to sharing NPS input contrasts with other businesses:

> "Most companies aggregate NPS results with additional business performance results and share NPS findings during divisional or company-wide meetings held monthly or quarterly. That information is muddled and delayed. Also, from a cultural perspective, many companies set a tone where senior managers risk embarrassment by releasing information on NPS performance to people outside their area. As such, those managers are either reluctant to share NPS results or spend a lot of time providing context or justifying the information they share."

By comparison, David emphasizes the power of and rationale for Macquarie's high level of NPS transparency:

> "By providing results to team members in real-time, they can self-calibrate. Suppose a customer

> rates a service interaction as a 7 on the net promoter question. The team members who provided that service can immediately reflect on what they could have done differently to create an experience that would have resulted in the customer being a promoter. Similarly, when a team member gets a 10, they can analyze behaviors contributing to that score. By publishing data within departments, people see their NPS performance stacked against peers. For most people, that activates personal pride, competitive spirit, or a desire to perform in alignment with colleagues so they contribute equitably to departmental and organizational goals."

Sitting in the Cloud Services contact center (the HMC) and listening to Macquarie engineers serve customers, the instantaneous nature of NPS feedback struck me, as did the speed with which NPS results refreshed on a prominent screen in front of this team of engineers. After completing a service interaction and having her NPS score posted, I asked HMC engineer Simone Bray to share her reaction to Macquarie's immediate and transparent approach to customer input. Simone noted:

> "We learn and grow by embracing feedback. At Macquarie, the experiences we provide are evaluated by our customers, and we are accountable to each other when it comes to maintaining an extraordinarily high standard of service excellence. I welcome that transparency."

Rewarding NPS performance – Legends and short-term team incentives

John E. Jones III is credited with saying, "What gets measured gets done. What gets measured and fed back gets done well. What gets rewarded gets repeated."

We've looked at Macquarie's measurement and feedback loops. Now, let's explore how NPS success is rewarded at Macquarie across individual, departmental, and organizational levels through the "Legends" program and by connecting NPS to broader KPIs.

Macquarie's Legends program recognizes team members who receive ten consecutive customer scores of ten on the net promoter question. This daunting bar means a team member is producing ten consecutive promoters and is doing so at the highest level of performance. Naveen adds, "Those who reach NPS 'Legend' status are recognized in their respective team meetings and celebrated at our quarterly Town Hall events. They also receive gift certificates in appreciation for their accomplishment."

In addition to recognition as an NPS Legend, Macquarie raises the bar even further by creating a performance status called the "League of Legends." To be inducted into the League of Legends, a team member must achieve Legend status *ten times in one year.* To recap, a team member who registers ten consecutive net promoter tens is a Legend. Someone who is a Legend ten times in a year joins the League of Legends.

In the decade since Macquarie launched the League of Legends, eight employees have met the highly challenging criteria for induction. In appreciation for those accomplishments, Macquarie provides inductees with an expenses-paid excursion of their choice. Only one team member, Finn Sheridan, has met League of Legends criteria twice. As you'll recall from Chapter 4, Finn was the "humble, hungry, and smart" newly recruited university graduate cited in a 2014 *Sydney Morning Herald* article.

When asked about Macquarie's Legends and League of Legends programs, Finn noted:

> "These are outstanding initiatives because they keep us focused on delivering the best experience possible for our customers while encouraging healthy competition. These recognition and reward programs also drive behavior and feed our hunger to achieve goals. As an engineer at Macquarie, I want to develop my technical skills. I also want to stretch my ability to delight customers through my service competency."

When asked about his travel rewards, Finn responded:

> "The incentive trips have been amazing, one of which enabled me to visit my girlfriend in London and travel with her across Europe. The other enabled my girlfriend to visit me and travel in Australia through Cairns and the Sunshine Coast. I couldn't be more grateful for the opportunity to serve customers and to be given these travel experiences as part of my efforts. This is just a part of what keeps me at Macquarie."

While Legends and the League of Legends inspire individual NPS performance, Macquarie also links NPS team goals to financial incentives. As mentioned in Chapter 5, everyone at Macquarie is expected to contribute to net sales performance, EBITDA, and NPS (the three boundaries in the "freedom within boundaries" model). Naveen explains how NPS fits into Macquarie's incentives:

> "Team performance on NPS contributes to 20 percent of our STI – or 'short term incentive' – performance on company profitability, and net sales make up the remainder of our bonus structure. That 20 percent NPS component is earned when teams meet their collective experience KPI."

Macquarie has consistently improved the company's overall NPS through dogged execution. David notes:

> "We started our NPS journey with a company average of +14 and quickly identified processes and systems issues that needed to be addressed centrally to drive customer engagement – like checking a new client's contract before sending them their first invoice. When we found ourselves stuck in the +30 to +35 range, the whole company missed its NPS bonus for two half-year periods, and we focused on empowering team managers to drive NPS. We needed a more refined, local, and targeted approach. Essentially, we had to move from painting with rollers to handheld brushes."

Since then, Macquarie's average NPS has been in the +70 to +80 range. Those scores are world-class and wildly uncharacteristic of the telecom sector. In an article for *Experience Benchmarks* titled "Telecom NPS Benchmarks and

CX Trends in 2022," Cvetilena Gocheva writes, "The telecommunications industry has long underperformed in customer experience with B2B and B2C clients alike. With a Net Promoter Score® average of 31, telecom holds the lowest industry average according to our latest NPS® Benchmarks Report." In that same report, IT companies averaged 40 on the NPS.

Practice your magic

1. How are you using each of the following to drive customer experience excellence:
    a. real-time feedback
    b. data transparency
    c. personal pride
    d. competitive spirit
    e. team alignment and accountability?

2. What programs have you established to reward and recognize individuals who consistently deliver excellent customer experiences?

3. How do you incentivize group performance towards customer experience goals?

4. Describe the customer experience journey of your department or company. Have you made consistent progress? If so, how would you prove that progress has occurred?

5. Can you benchmark your customer experience against other companies in your industry? If so, how do you perform? If not, how can you measure customer experience in a way that enables comparison within your industry and beyond?

NPS and performance

The NPS generates tangible returns that justify the time and attention Macquarie leaders invest. David Tudehope notes:

> "Our data and business performance show that happy customers stay with us longer, buy more from Macquarie, and refer their friends and colleagues. Happy customers also pay their bills faster than those who are merely satisfied. NPS is our tool for assessing customer happiness and inspiring everyone in our organization to drive exceptional experiences."

Figure 5: NPS results

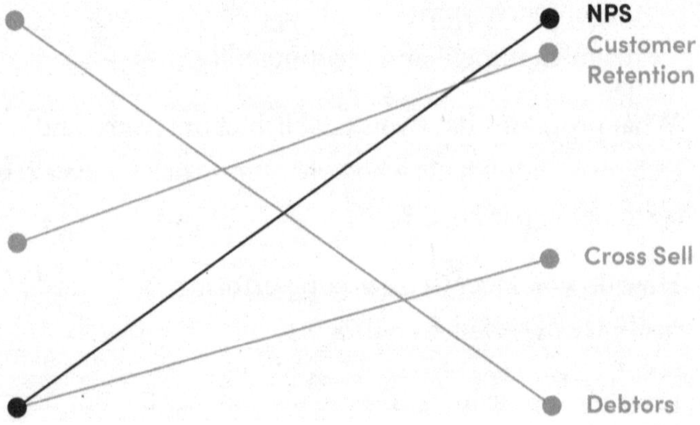

When I shared with Fred Reichheld how Macquarie's NPS performance correlates with customer retention, cross-sell, and swift payments, he responded:

> "I have not yet found a company that can consistently deliver outstanding shareholder value that

> does not do a better job than competitors at making customers happy. That is because the economic flywheel that drives cash generation is this: happy customers come back for more and refer their friends. Companies that benefit from this flywheel don't have to buy growth; they earn it. Earning growth provides the only economically sustainable formula."

Naveen Gera, Head of Service Assurance, reports that the NPS inspires him to ensure that every customer he serves is a Macquarie promoter. For example, Naveen shared a service story involving Macquarie's customer Experian (a credit bureau serving clients in approximately 100 countries):

> "A leader at Experian reached out to our HMC on a Saturday morning noting that their service was down. That call escalated to me. As I researched the situation, I determined that a third-party vendor came to one of our data centers and decommissioned some of Experian's equipment. I tracked down Experian's vendor to advise them that they had disrupted a service that was supposed to be in use. The vendor insisted that he acted at the request of Experian and that his team would take it up with Experian at another time. I tried to persuade the vendor to return to our data center and reverse what he had done so Experian could resume processing credit inquiries. He advised me that he was on another job and his soonest return time would be nine hours. Even though Macquarie wasn't responsible for servicing the Experian equipment, I asked the vendor to tell

me where he was so I could go to him, get the equipment, and reinstall it."

Upon returning to the data center with the equipment, Naveen reached out to his Experian contact. He asked them to look for any documents or network diagrams that would help him with reinstallation. About 90 minutes after Naveen returned to the data center, all Experian services were operational. Naveen adds:

> "I was pleased that Experian customers could get their credit checked to buy cars or other products. Macquarie's commitment to customer experience excellence inspires me to go above and beyond for our customers, even when it's supposedly 'not my job.' I want every customer I work with to advocate for and promote Macquarie. I also want those customers to create success for those they serve."

Naveen's service story and Macquarie's overall approach to customer loyalty and advocacy are best summarized by the late Walt Disney, who suggested, "Whatever you do, do it well. Do it so well that when people see you do it, they will want to come back and see you do it again, and they will want to bring others and show them how well you do what you do."

To help ensure your organization's repeat business and customer referrals, let's do a quick review.

Make your difference

- Customer experience excellence often requires a willingness to benchmark against competitors and world-class experience brands.
- Customer satisfaction surveys are often long and complicated, yielding low response rates and ambiguous insights that are difficult to activate.
- According to decades of research by Fred Reichheld and colleagues at Bain & Company, business growth can best be predicted by asking customers, "How likely are you [on a 0-to-10 scale] to recommend [company X] to a friend or colleague?"
- The Net Promoter System (NPS) involves asking customers a "likelihood to recommend" question and categorizing respondents as either "detractors" (0 through 6), "passives" (7 or 8) or "promoters" (9 or 10), and subtracting the percentage of detractors from the percentage of promoters.
- The NPS recommends closing the internal feedback loop by sharing results with service providers and completing the external feedback loop by seeking customer resolution.
- Effective use of customer feedback involves responding to issues raised by a specific customer and looking for ways to use that feedback to avert problems for others.
- World-class customer experience brands like Macquarie ensure team members receive real-time customer

feedback and publish customer input in ways that inspire personal responsibility and constructive competition.

- What gets measured gets done. What gets rewarded gets repeated.
- Look for ways to reward and incentivise individuals and groups to meet customer experience objectives.
- Explore customer experience metrics that allow you to compare your business with others in and outside your industry.
- Happy customers stay longer, buy more, refer their friends or colleagues, and pay their bills faster.

Chapter 7
A Noah's Ark of Innovation

"One man's 'magic' is another man's engineering."
Robert Heinlein

Harvard Business School Professor Stefan Thomke and professional magician Jason Randal have spent years examining the connection between magic and innovation. Thomke and Randal report that professional magicians work within tight budgets to innovate new illusions or "effects" that will create memorable and magical customer experiences. Magicians purportedly apply a systemic top-down and bottom-up innovation process to achieve their goals. They ask top-down questions like "What problem am I trying to solve?" and "What effect am I trying to achieve?" Similarly, they ask bottom-up questions like "Who has successfully solved similar problems?" and "What existing processes or techniques can I deploy or improve?"

In an article for *The European Business Review*, Thomke

and Randal describe problem definition as "often the most underrated part of the innovation process." Though it is often overlooked by managers, "Savvy companies have learned to spend the proper attention to problem definition way upstream in the innovation process. They carefully observe customers, learn from lead users, and tap into other sources of information that help them frame the problem correctly." They also know that part of the "magic" of a successful product comes from going beyond just meeting needs to solve problems in unexpected ways that enhance the total customer experience.

In this chapter, you will learn about a unique innovation process developed by David and Aidan Tudehope, which Macquarie's leaders use to define problems, observe customers, and tap into other sources of information. This methodology, which David refers to as the "Noah's Ark" approach, has enabled Macquarie to assess, evaluate, select, and implement successful business solutions optimized for Macquarie's core market. Before diving into the who and how of Noah's Ark and the many breakthroughs Macquarie has derived from it, let's explore its origin.

Building the ark

In Macquarie's start-up phase, David and Aidan Tudehope faced top-down and bottom-up questions like "What do we need to do to succeed as a small business in an industry overshadowed by a dominant legacy provider?" and "What have others done to achieve success under similar circumstances?" To answer these questions, David and Aidan traveled to the US to learn from leaders at companies who had battled the US's legacy service provider. One of the companies David and Aidan visited was MCI.

About ten years before Macquarie faced off with Telstra, MCI initiated its telecom war with telecom monopoly AT&T. In *Forbes' Greatest Business Stories of All Time*, Daniel Gross describes the MCI versus AT&T battle in a way that sounds strikingly similar to the Macquarie versus Telstra conflict outlined in Chapter 2. Like Telstra, AT&T held a government-regulated monopoly: "By 1967 its budget was larger than that of a small European country; its assets exceeded those of Standard Oil, General Motors, Ford, and IBM combined. AT&T was the paragon of American industry, the largest private-sector employer in the nation, and the issuer of its most widely held stock." MCI, meanwhile, was "a tiny company with a handful of employees and no revenue." However, they had a visionary CEO, Bill McGowan, who aimed to break up AT&T's monopoly over the US telecommunications industry and establish competition – and, through a decades-long duel, he did just that.

Since that initial trip, David and Aidan developed a unique process that has fueled visits to hundreds of telecom and technology companies over Macquarie's 30-year history. Aidan explains these "innovation study trips," the Noah's Ark approach, by noting:

> "Through the years, we've developed discipline around innovation study trips. We've systematized how frequently we take them, how we craft our areas of inquiry, which companies to visit, whom to send on them, and the processes needed for making innovation decisions when we return."

Choosing the research question or problem definition

IBM founder Thomas J. Watson suggested, "The ability to ask the right question is more than half the battle of finding the answer." In that vein, Macquarie's leaders use the company's overarching objectives to decide which topics and trends they will study. This process ensures that study teams are addressing the *right* questions.

Aidan notes:

> "Keeping our long-range objectives in mind, leaders of our business units engage in business-case presentations and robust discussion about the questions we need to explore. We plan between two and four innovation trips annually to evaluate trends and opportunities likely to have the greatest impact on Macquarie's customers and business success. Sometimes we look for insights on how to meet an existing goal better. Most of the time, however, we evaluate how to benefit from emerging trends or innovations. We avoid the 'spray and pray' strategy and seek sniper-like precision on our innovation targets. We are a company that invests in a limited number of major projects as opposed to many small ones, so we always make sure our potential investments of time and money will be manageable before committing to a particular trip."

Before an innovation study excursion, team members spend weeks refining their questions and conducting extensive research on the topics or technologies they will explore.

Given the ultra-rapid pace of technology advancements, Macquarie's leaders use these innovation trips to decipher fads from trends. They want to sort the "signal from the noise" and the "shiny object from lasting solution." They also assess the relevance and likely adoption of the technologies under study for their middle-to-large Australian business customers.

Choosing the ark's passengers and destination

As you've likely guessed, these innovation study trips acquired the name "Noah's Ark" based on the diversity of the Macquarie team members who participated. David describes the selection process by noting, "We make sure the people chosen for these trips come from disparate roles so that we can get differing perspectives on the same problem or issue."

On average, Macquarie brings five to eight team members and picks them from the business units most relevant to the inquiry. James Mystakidis, the Group Executive for Macquarie Cloud

Services, reports:

> "Some trips will focus on issues exclusive to a single business unit like Cloud, Government or Telecom, while others will overlap multiple telecom and technology areas. Study trips tend to be funded by the business units that will benefit most from the insights gained."

Aidan offers an example of the type of team that embarks on these trips:

> "We don't just bring a CEO and a board member. Instead, we have a mix of senior leaders, salespeople, engineers, product managers, and system architects. Because we are a technology company, we tend to be weighted in favor of people who can understand the nuances of the technology under consideration. We find that high-level technology concepts and the potential benefits of those technologies are understood easily. However, it takes engineering expertise to understand and evaluate subtle but relevant details that affect the technology's viability for our customers."

Aidan also views these trips as a development opportunity for high-potential team members: "In addition to our core team, we frequently give an up-and-coming employee a chance to travel, learn, and take responsibility for many of the actions needed to maintain momentum when we return."

After deciding on key questions, Macquarie's leaders reach out to companies in overseas markets who can share relevant experiences and insights. Aidan notes:

> "We love visiting customers of providers similar to us as well as government entities and technology companies. We tend to avoid vendors and executive briefing centers (EBCs) that focus on corporate rhetoric or product-related talking points. We learn a lot when the hosting team includes founders, chief technology officers, pre-sale engineers or experienced account directors anchored in the business. We generally want to meet with people with commercial expertise and significant customer contact."

Before we get into a detailed description of Macquarie's on-site visits and examine the benefits that Macquarie derives from them, let's apply some of this Noah's Ark process.

Practice your magic

1. Do you agree with Thomas J. Watson's perspective that "the ability to ask the right question is more than half the battle of finding the answer"? If so, why? If not, why not?
2. Stefan Thomke and Jason Randal describe problem definition as "often the most underrated part of the innovation process" and something that many companies do not pay close enough attention to. To what degree is this true for innovation initiated by you, your department or your organization?
3. What top-down questions help define your innovation opportunities? (For example, "What problem am I trying to solve?")
4. What bottom-up questions guide your innovation process? (For example, "What existing processes or techniques can I deploy or improve?")
5. Discuss examples of when well-crafted problem definitions helped achieve practical solutions or poorly crafted definitions failed to create breakthroughs.
6. Do you, your department or your organisation have something similar to Macquarie's Noah's Ark process? If so, how are study questions defined? How are study participants selected? How frequently do your innovation tours occur? What companies do you visit? If you don't have an innovation study trip process, what questions

would you like answered? How might you select participants? Ideally, how frequently would you arrange these visits? What companies would you like to visit?

The on-site experience

Thus far, you've learned that a diverse team of Macquarie leaders and employees spends weeks researching technologies of interest and preparing for their meetings with hosts in overseas markets. But what happens when the team arrives on-site?

Aidan Tudehope answers:

> "Our trip length is usually two weeks. After we settle in, we have multiple visits a day, Monday through Friday, with host businesses or agencies. Over two weeks, we usually study a couple of dozen different entities. These meetings occur in a mixture of formal and informal settings. For example, we love it when a team joins us for lunch or dinner after an office meeting because that informality frequently results in rich takeaways. We're also keen to ensure we are sharing and providing value. Informal settings give us more time to answer our hosts' questions and offer insights of interest to them. We also want to help them think differently about their business."

On average, each Macquarie site visit lasts 90 minutes, and Macquarie team members are mentally exhausted by the time they share dinner each workday evening. Saturdays are "workshop days" when, according to Aidan:

> "Our team discusses the information from the prior week. If it's the end of the first week, we plan for upcoming visits. Usually, we try to do a group activity on Saturday nights to capture the unique aspects of the city we are visiting. During our last Saturday workshop, we assimilate findings from all meetings, define and delegate our next steps, and book follow-up meetings for when we return home."

Before we explore the decision-making process that occurs when the study teams get back to Australia, let's consider David's perspective on what makes these trips particularly productive:

> "There is something magical that happens when we travel to other countries. We are immersed in planning, observing, listening, and inquiring about technologies and solutions that typically prove useful for our customers. Because we are usually in time zones that don't align with the Australian workday, we can stay focused on our information-finding mission. We eat together, socialize, and pay unwavering attention to the business questions at hand."

Participants in these meetings report leaving the study sessions with notebooks full of insights. Moreover, the study teams indicate that participant role diversity helps them find different pieces of the puzzle they are trying to solve. David puts it this way: "An engineer's takeaway might be that the company under study jumped from software version 1.0 to 3.0 without having to transition through version 2.0, while a salesperson might focus on a differentiator that drives conversion in that market."

Returning home

Francis Bacon opined that "knowledge is power," and Macquarie's innovation groups certainly returned to Australia having acquired an overwhelming amount of knowledge. However, does knowledge alone empower innovation? Or is it true, as Dale Carnegie suggests, that "knowledge isn't power until it is applied"?

To activate the knowledge Macquarie teams gather during innovation trips, team members reconvene upon their return, conduct follow-up calls, and prepare a business case showing the proposed technology's costs and benefits. Depending upon the scope and the investment required, the business case is presented to leaders at a business unit level or Macquarie's entire leadership team.

It's important to note that some study trips help Macquarie determine that a technological solution is *unsuitable* for their customers. For example, David shares:

> "We studied a popular trend toward IP telephony. IP telephony involves moving from the customer-based telephone equipment of the last 100 years to functionality inside the telecom carrier network. During our trip, we explored different presentations of this technology and determined that these solutions are popular with small business customers. For example, Gamma PLC has greatly succeeded with these offerings throughout the United Kingdom. Since the UK is often considered a country of small businesses

and shopkeepers, these technologies were perfect for that market.

"When we returned from our study trip, we spent months examining the business case for these products. We debated whether we should try to reach out to small business owners in Australia and offer this solution. Ultimately, we decided that Gamma's success with small business customers was based on a UK market dynamic of many small telecom resellers that sold to other local small businesses. That market dynamic didn't exist in Australia. Instead, we decided to launch only a supplementary offering targeted to customers with large numbers of small sites like traditional retailers."

As an innovation tool, David notes:

"One test of these study tours is whether you sometimes conclude that you shouldn't embrace a new technology. We have done this several times due to the absence of small business resellers in our market, or the concentration of banks limiting the opportunities. More importantly, the ultimate test of this approach is how it has guided us to breakthrough opportunities."

Game-changing innovation

David credits the Noah's Ark process for fueling all of Macquarie's major innovations:

"These study trips are one of the most significant elements of Macquarie's magic. They provide a unique platform *to ensure a company is agile and embraces mission-critical opportunities.* Everything we've done in our cloud, cyber, and data centers is directly linked to these trips. When we started, we were 100 percent telecom. Because we've effectively evaluated viable trends for our market, we are now 10 percent telecom and 90 percent technology companies.

"We built a $30 million data center in Sydney in 2000 because a Noah's Ark trip showed us that US customers were moving their data centers out of their corporate offices. From today's vantage point, the choice to build a data center might seem obvious. However, before that trip, no one had built one in Australia. The findings from that US visit gave us confidence that we were anticipating an emerging, unserved need. I recall presenting at a telecom conference that data centers would change our industry like Edison's central power plants had replaced company-owned generators housed near their offices and factories 100 years before. At the time of my presentation, telecom companies were dismissing data centers as niche offerings for e-commerce companies, viewing them as irrelevant to the needs of 'serious businesses' that needed the IT room to be near their IT staff in the head office. Our first data center, like all the others we've built, are game-changers in keeping with our purpose to make a difference for markets that are underserved and overcharged."

If you're in a large technology business or work in a rapidly changing industry, it's easy to see how innovation study trips can create breakthroughs, but does this process apply to smaller businesses or other sectors? David is convinced it does:

"The key is *not* to get trapped in your ecosystem. For example, let's assume a restaurant owner is successful in a given town. They may rely on their chef to innovate new offerings and occasionally find time to visit nearby restaurants. The idea behind our type of innovation is to be strategic about getting ahead of trends and evaluating the viability of those trends in your market. Applying our innovation model to a restaurant owner might involve regularly scheduled visits to other regions and countries. On those trips, the owner could bring various team members like chefs, managers, and frontline staff to explore possibilities."

Practice your magic

1. What stands out about the way Macquarie teams spend time when they are abroad? What factors contribute to their ability to gather the information they need successfully?

2. How do you, your department, or your business use acquired knowledge to power innovation?

3. More specifically, what processes do you deploy to evaluate the costs and benefits of opportunities?

4. Apple CEO Steve Jobs said, "Focusing is about saying no." Think about and share examples of when you, your department, or your company said "no" to a seemingly profitable opportunity because it didn't fit your goals, resources, or core customer needs. Are there similar examples of when your focus drifted and you said "yes" when you shouldn't have?

5. Based on Macquarie's approach to innovation study tours and David's example from the restaurant sector, explore and discuss how you can adapt the Noah's Ark approach to drive breakthrough innovations strategically.

David Tudehope describes the technology sector as "validating Darwin's observation that it's not the strongest of the species that survive, nor the most intelligent, but the ones that are most responsive to change. Specifically, in telecom and technology, today's roosters turn into tomorrow's feather dusters." While I expand on this observation in great detail in Chapter 9 (in the context of Macquarie's three-decade history as a technology leader), David's point conjures images of failed technology companies that were lauded as the next big thing. Their names appeared on billboards and atop buildings in places like Silicon Valley, Seattle, Shanghai, and Sydney.

A failure to innovate is a harbinger of disaster for most businesses, not just those in tech. In a *Harvard Business Review* article, Gary Hamel describes this risk by ominously noting, "Out there in some garage is an entrepreneur who's forging a bullet with your company's name on it. You've got one option now – to shoot first. You've got to out-innovate the innovators." Many try to meet the challenge of "out-innovating the innovators" by creating "never seen before" solutions. Macquarie's innovation approach always aligns with the company's purpose and is optimized for its customers. Sometimes innovation means being first to market with new technology like data centers and SD-WAN. Other times innovation involves adapting technology to better meet the needs of Macquarie's target market.

In *Winning Through Innovation: A Practical Guide to Leading Organizational Change and Renewal*, Harvard Business School Professor Michael L. Tushman (who also wrote the foreword for *Customer Magic*) and Stanford Business Professor Charles A. O'Reilly notes how, when a new product or service is gaining acceptance, "Successful companies learn what works well and incorporate this knowledge into their operations. During periods of evolutionary change, managers engage in continuous, incremental change – constantly refining the organization to better accomplish its mission ... The overall system adapts."

Macquarie's Noah's Ark reflects a continuously improving process to "learn what works well" for the company's customers and refine how leaders innovate to better "accomplish Macquarie's mission." It is customer magic at its best.

Make your difference

- To achieve your innovation goals, apply a systemic top-down and bottom-up process.
- Problem definition is the most underrated and essential part of innovation.
- Savvy companies attend to problem definition upstream in the innovation process.
- Innovation study tours define problems, observe customers, and tap into rich sources of information.
- Macquarie uses its innovation study tours (the Noah's Ark approach) to assess, evaluate, select, and implement successful business solutions optimized for its core market.
- To effectively understand emerging trends, assemble a team of people from diverse roles and with diverse perspectives.
- Focus on a few of the most promising trends before studying others.
- Reach out to and schedule meetings with solution providers and customers of those providers who are outside your geographic market.
- When possible, structure your innovation study tours to be immersive and remove your team from their day-to-day responsibilities.
- During tours, have the team discuss and assimilate insights. Assign next steps and schedule follow-up meetings.

- Since you will likely acquire considerable knowledge during innovation trips, remember Dale Carnegie's warning that "knowledge isn't power until it is applied."
- Reconvene after your trip, conduct follow-up calls and prepare a business case showing the costs and benefits of the proposed technology or solution.
- In keeping with Steve Jobs's view that "focusing is about saying no," be willing to say "no" to opportunities that aren't optimized for your customers or business competencies.
- Be strategic and consistently invest in processes like innovation study tours to help you spot trends and respond to your customers' emerging needs.

Chapter 8
Zigging when Others Zag

"If you want seemingly magical business success, determine when to veer off the well-worn path."
John Yokoyama

Throughout my work with Macquarie, I've frequently heard David Tudehope, Macquarie's CEO, talk about "zigging when others zag." Initially, I assumed David was referencing unconventional choices he and other leaders at Macquarie have made throughout the years. Interpreting "zigging and zagging" from my perspective, I concluded that all the following actions (covered in previous chapters) were examples of zigging when others zag:

- David and Aidan Tudehope taking the path of tireless personal and professional growth, including coaching, reading and actively reaching out to their professional networks
- the way the founders adapted to and stewarded Macquarie

through varied developmental challenges how the founders crafted an actionable purpose and succinct values

- the way Macquarie's cultural infrastructure guides decision making and behavior
- how Macquarie's leaders maintain their investments in tools such as the Heartbeat program to ensure storytelling reinforces the purpose and values
- Macquarie's leadership telling recently graduated engineers that their first job at Macquarie will begin with a grueling two-year program of learning and rewards
- how Macquarie puts commitments for career development and certifications in writing, along with related pay increases
- the fact that Macquarie leaders created an EVP that includes career paths extending a decade past a new hire's initial contract
- how Macquarie leaders pursue "freedom within boundaries" and align business units around customer experience, growth, and profitability goals
- the way leaders use the NPS as a disciplined real-time customer listening tool
- leadership's response to internal and external feedback loops, which resolve specific customer issues, refine processes, innovate solutions, anticipate customer needs, build new products, and deliver world-class results
- finally, the way Macquarie leaders created a novel Noah's Ark approach for benchmarking and innovation, which has guided all market-relevant investments.

Later in this chapter, I will expand on examples of what I now call "road less travele'" behavior, but first, let's look at

David Tudehope's more nuanced view of what it means to zig when others zag.

When David speaks about zigging and zagging, he explicitly discusses *delivering on a promise framed by Macquarie's purpose.* While competitors underserve and overcharge (zag), Macquarie accentuates service and makes pricing decisions based on value delivery (zig). Across Macquarie, the concept of zigging when others zag is commonly thought of as *making choices with the customer's best interest in mind* and *trusting that customer-centricity will lead to sustained business success and growth.*

Adding "un" to messaging and process

In keeping with David's definition of zigging and zagging, Macquarie markets itself as a renegade service brand. For example, Macquarie's Telecom business unit uses the hashtag "#SoUntelco" and invites prospective customers to compare Macquarie's to "old-school" telecom companies (where service is veritably non-existent).

Luke Clifton, who worked for one of those "old-school" competitors (Telstra) for more than a decade and is now a 12-year veteran and Group Executive for Macquarie Telecom, notes:

> "We truly are "#SoUntelco." It is more than a slogan or marketing campaign. It is our approach to business. At every management meeting, I ask three questions. First, what have our competitors done recently? Second, what would it look like if we did the complete opposite? Finally, how can we ensure that our oppositional approach will meet our customers' needs and drive profitability?"

Ash Fogwill, a Project Manager on Macquarie Telecom's service delivery team, shares what #SoUntelco means to her and her frontline colleagues:

> "Unlike our competitors, I focus on making a personal connection with the customers I serve and not just ticking boxes to complete a transaction. To highlight this distinction, a competitor received a frantic call from a customer noting that a car had just crashed into their business, and they needed their phones diverted. Our competitor's immediate response was to ask to which number they wanted the calls sent. At Macquarie, our immediate response would have been to ask if everyone was okay before addressing the transactional need."

While impersonal approaches might be more productive, Ash indicates that building relationships enhances productivity:

> "My job is to turn on services for customers rapidly. Expediting service initiation is good for our customers and good for us. While speed is critical, so is getting to know my customers and helping them succeed. For example, I turned on 250 sites for a customer within six months, which smashed her goal and ensured she achieved a performance incentive from her company. Throughout that process, she and I talked about topics like our kids – she has twins, and I had my first child – and home improvement projects."

Ash shared another example of relationship building:

"In my role, I don't typically resolve technical issues, but when I heard that a customer felt uncomfortable plugging in an ethernet cable, I asked if I could stop by in the morning to assist her. She replied, 'I'll need coffee at that time in the morning,' so I brought her one when I helped her with the cable. Humanizing service doesn't take much effort; we all want to be treated as people, not transactions. For my colleagues and me, being #SoUntelco means providing quality products delivered personally and expeditiously."

One of Ash's colleagues, Bill Gaw (Client Director, strategic accounts at Macquarie Telecom), adds:

"We are #SoUntelco by acting with urgency for our clients when competitors wait to have a 'ticket raised.' We track issues through a service ticket but don't postpone our response because a ticket hasn't been raised. Instead, we act based on our client's needs and raise a ticket on their behalf if they haven't logged one."

Luke Clifton expands on Bill's example by noting:

"To be effective, my team 'zigs' by staying clear of bureaucratic traps commonplace in the telecom industry. We streamline decision-making to meet customer needs without excessive levels of approval. We separate ourselves from the telecom pack by fending off organizational behavior that zaps the spirit of employees and strains customer relationships."

Macquarie customers such as Jeff Vanasse, Global Program Management Officer of Perfecto (a company that provides secure mobile and web testing in the cloud), are quick to offer examples of Macquarie's elevated service and added value, in keeping with David Tudehope's definition of zigging when others zag.

Jeff notes:

> "We deploy six data centers globally, one of which is a Macquarie data center in Sydney. In each of these data centers, we have racks of cell phones on which our customers are testing their apps in a real-world environment. This testing requires 24/7 coverage in the data centers. When a problem occurs, we open a ticket, and the Macquarie team has to find the right device from about 100 and get that phone back online as quickly as possible. Unlike any of our other data center partners, Macquarie team members took the initiative to develop a stand that our devices sit on. Those proactive efforts have changed how we've set up our racks. Other than actual material costs, Macquarie didn't charge us for that new rack development. This is just one example of how Macquarie elevates service in ways other data centers don't, and Macquarie's unconventional service makes a difference for us."

In addition to lacking proactivity, Jeff notes that most data centers struggle to accommodate his company's needs:

> "For example, we decided to send laptops to each of our data centers to enable faster back-and-forth

communication from our team to the data center staff. Macquarie was one of two data centers that immediately began using our preferred communication channel, and it's been a challenge to get the other four on board. Macquarie creates value through outstanding uptime, responsiveness, accommodation to our preferred communication channel, and proactive service. All of that sets them apart in the cloud service industry."

Now that you've seen how Macquarie delivers on David Tudehope's customer-centric definition of zigging and zagging, let's look at how Macquarie leaders take what I now call "the road less traveled."

Leading on the road less traveled

While Macquarie leaders strive to expedite service delivery. and leadership decision-making, they don't shy away from spirited discourse. David suggests why unconventional ideas surface:

> "Because diverse executives engage in constructive, open and vigorous debate grounded in data and analytics. I've observed many leadership teams and am surprised by their lack of healthy, evidence-based discussion. Without that discourse, teams fail to generate and test ideas. In those low-engagement teams, few disagreements surface, and divergent thought is squelched or handled in private conversations. By contrast, our leadership team creates an environment of respect and trust where colleagues

> are valued for challenging conventional thinking, leveraging data, and tamping down confirmation biases."

Macquarie's leadership team successfully deploys consensus-based decision-making – even though, to David's point, that approach often renders less-than-optimal results for other organizations. In a *Harvard Business Review* article, Jennifer Mueller, Sarah Harvey, and Alec Levenson note, "Research shows that consensus-based problem-solving groups are often where innovative ideas go to die. These groups are highly prone to groupthink – quick agreement around status quo solutions with little discussion or deliberation."

High-performance team builder Dr. Pete Stebbins suggests that groupthink "is real and an important part of understanding why teams fail. The antidote is, of course, a commitment to objective evaluation, seeking data and evidence to inform decisions, and encouraging and respecting people in the team with contrarian views."

Tony Pandher, Chief Operations Officer at Macquarie Cloud Services, describes the interactional style of Macquarie's executive team as "challenging":

> "The team pushes one another to be their best. I think we are more about alignment than consensus. We don't rush to an agreement just to get on with business. We work through disagreements and explore what it will take to support one another. For example, someone might say, 'I can't accept or align with that course of action, but if we modify this one element, I'm all in.'"

David Tudehope adds:

> "The Macquarie executive team is very diverse in style, and our meetings are characterized by diverse thinking. Business ideas are rigorously tested, and our direct culture supports robust discussions. We avoid presentations and ask that documents be sent for pre-reading at least 48 hours before a meeting. We expect documents to be read in advance to expedite discussions and decision-making. Final decisions require agreement from all six executives, and on rare occasions, we seek the Board's agreement. At the end of every meeting, we ask everyone if we 'moved the ball forward' or 'made the boat go faster.'"

As an example of when the diverse thinking of the leadership team moves the ball forward, David shares:

> "We recently reviewed a business case for a new cybersecurity product, and there was a vigorous debate about the size of the market, competing products that were more successful than the business case recognized and whether the operational processes were ready. All of these elements the sponsoring executive accepted were valuable perspectives, and as a result, the business case was amended significantly and approved two months later."

In short, Macquarie's leadership team takes the road less traveled regarding spirited and idea-generating meetings. In the process, that team produces business-advancing results.

Challenging false choice

Typically, business decisions involve "either-or" options. At Macquarie, however, executives challenge whether a choice is even required. For example, do leaders need to choose either operational excellence *or* disruptive innovation?

David notes:

> "We won't choose between executing flawlessly or aggressively pursuing game-changing innovation. We see that as a 'false choice' and prefer to take a disciplined and balanced approach that we call 'strategic innovation.' We exercise restraint when pursuing too many exciting new ideas until our in-progress innovations are completed. For us, spectacular execution is as important as inspiring innovation. That spectacular execution extends from activating an idea to making that activation scalable."

David and other Macquarie leaders credit Harvard Business School Professor Michael L. Tushman for shaping their views on choosing the "and" over the "or" when facing false choices. Dr. Tushman, who has written several books and countless academic articles, builds his business approach on a platform he calls "ambidextrous leadership," which he and Charles A. O'Reilly describe in *Winning Through Innovation: A Practical Guide to Leading Organizational Change and Renewal.* Essentially, in those firms that enjoy the most long-term success, managers balance stability and incremental change on the one hand, and experimentation and discontinuous change on the other, creating the capacity for both present and future excellence.

James Mystakidis, Group Executive for Macquarie Cloud Services, likens Macquarie's leadership ambidexterity to "being able to play table tennis with both hands":

> "With the right hand, we're innovating, thinking strategically, and bringing new ideas into the business. With the left hand, we're operating the business and achieving world-class results. I think of ambidexterity as embracing innovation – both incremental and disruptive – while maintaining a maniacal focus on execution and performance."

David provides a tangible example of what ambidextrous leadership looks like at Macquarie:

> "When we looked to establish a new public cloud business that would likely partly cannibalize our existing, successful private cloud business, we decided that Group Executive James Mystakidis would need to manage this internal tension. We realized there was a risk that a successful existing business would become focused on limiting cannibalization rather than seizing the opportunity to grow the new business wherever there was demand. Then, after two years, we recognized that the new business and its manager had grown to the point where they could manage this tension successfully."

Another "and" – execute and share

In addition to ambidextrously executing and innovating, Macquarie leaders maintain operational excellence *and* share their learnings – especially regarding customer experience excellence. Macquarie's sharing process is similar to seldom-traveled paths taken by other world-class businesses.

After twice winning the Malcolm Baldrige National Quality Award for operational and customer experience excellence, leaders at The Ritz-Carlton Hotel Company launched the Ritz-Carlton Leadership Center to help others deliver extraordinary customer experiences. Similarly, Zappos, an online retailer known for its unconventional approach to company culture and service elevation, created a training team called "Zappos Insights" to help interested parties learn Zappos's approach to service delivery. Like Macquarie, leaders at The Ritz-Carlton Hotel Company and Zappos allowed me to share their stories in books titled *The New Gold Standard* and *The Zappos Experience*.

When I asked David if he had any reservations about sharing key learnings related to Macquarie's success, he noted:

> "I guess if a leader operates from the perspective of scarcity, they might see information sharing as a matter of 'us' versus 'them.' They'd likely keep their learnings to themself, hoping to insulate their business from competitive threats. However, we know the importance of learning from and teaching others. Our innovation tours reflect our commitment to reciprocal information sharing. We learn from our hosts and offer them our best practices, including insights on elevating customer experiences. I see this book, *Customer Magic*, as an extension of that commitment. Knowledge is a starting point for action, so why not share information with those willing to raise the customer experience bar?"

In addition to the knowledge-sharing Macquarie provides through this book and during innovation tours, leaders at Macquarie have formalized service culture training to help their customers excel. Head of Service Assurance Naveen Gera notes:

> "We train customers who are interested in learning how we deliver service. Our workshop content highlights Macquarie's customer experience journey and how the NPS changed us. We review the NPS methodology and how to apply it across all customer journey phases. We cover the importance of unbiased survey processes, ways to maximize response rates, and how to close feedback loops consistently. We also discuss our Heartbeat program and the results Macquarie achieves through our commitment to service. Finally, we leave ample time for questions."

Gifts are the topping

Gift-giving at Macquarie epitomizes a road-less-traveled business approach. David Tudehope sets the stage:

> "Close your eyes for a moment and think about your business telecom or cloud provider. Now imagine them sending you a personalized gift demonstrating their genuine interest in you. I am not talking about a free t-shirt at a conference, a cardboard sun visor or a balloon for a five-year-old. I am talking about a real gift. Imagine the gift is accompanied by a card that reads, 'Joseph, best wishes for the birth of your first child, and I would like to acknowledge

> how much I have enjoyed working with you over the last three months on the deployment of your cloud platform.'"

David's visualization exercise requires an overly active imagination – maybe even a willingness to engage in pure fantasy. However, Macquarie team members make David's scenario a reality by paying attention to their customers and personally acknowledging them. David continues using a cake analogy:

> "Doing your job in response to a customer's request is like the sponge of a cake. It is foundational, but you wouldn't sell many cakes if you owned a cake shop that only sold the sponge. Living our value of personal accountable service (PAS) puts the icing on the cake by exceeding customer expectations. For us, a thoughtful gift is like placing a sugar figurine with a celebratory message on top written in icing. It would be unappealing if you were to give someone a plate of icing or just the celebratory "Happy Birthday" message written by itself. By combining the expected sponge with the delight of the icing or frosting and then finishing with a thoughtful message on top, we create a beautiful cake that will live forever in people's memories. So, we aim to create experiences that will be remembered forever. Combining the three elements of doing the requested, laying over the expected personal accountable service, and finishing with a thoughtful gift with a handwritten message creates an experience that will be remembered long after, and we craft Macquarie magic."

Figure 6: The customer service cake

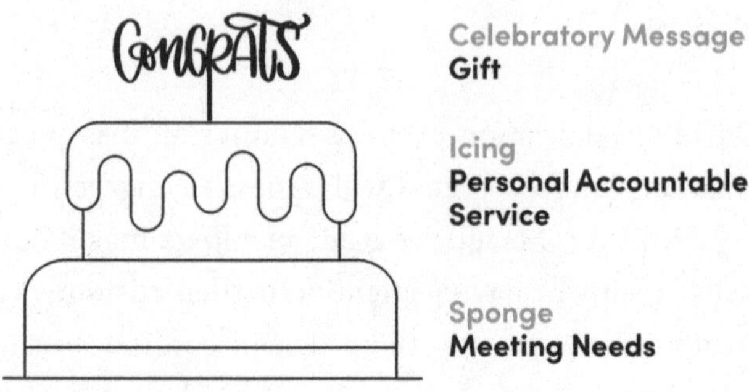

To appreciate what David means by a "tailored gift," here's an example from Aaron Tighe, State Manager for Macquarie in Western Australia. The gift recipients were Tony and Frankie Galati of Spudshed, a high-profile, family-owned fruit and vegetable farm in Western Australia. Tony is the business's founder and his son Frankie is the current CEO. As Spudshed's third anniversary with Macquarie approached, Aaron asked Tony from what part of Sicily his father emigrated. The answer was a small mountainside town called Tortorici. Aaron then arranged for a designer to produce two acrylic photo blocks – one for Tony and one for Frankie – depicting the picturesque town of Tortorici. Each gift was inscribed with a personal message of appreciation from the Macquarie team. When Aaron dropped off the gifts to Frankie, Spudshed's CEO was positively surprised and acknowledged that he was "wowed." Aaron explained, "This was a small token of appreciation for their support over the past three years – a nice way to say thank you." This tailored gift reflected Macquarie's sincerity and personal authenticity in keeping with David's example. It was comparable to a sugar figurine atop colorful icing on a delectable cake.

While Macquarie acknowledges personal and business milestones, team members don't send generic cards or gifts on recognized holidays and are careful about using gifts in service recovery. David notes, "Like every business, we drop the ball sometimes. Customers naturally expect us to fix the issue, and we must endeavor to demonstrate Personal-Accountability service. If we do this, a small gift with a handwritten card can reinforce that we are genuinely sorry."

While gift-giving seems straightforward, David reports that he made mistakes while trying to empower team members to send tailored gifts:

> "When we started the gifting program, we set it up so that our people could give any dollar value of gift without approval. That approach was wrong, as the dollar value was too open-ended and the type of gift so wide that our people weren't sure what was appropriate. As a result, few gifts were given. Over time, we refined the program to give more curated options at different levels of value to allow them to choose the best fit for each opportunity while maintaining ample team member freedom to select gifts that connect personally with their recipients."

How often do you hear a CEO admit that their approach was "wrong" or "too open-ended?" Similarly, reflecting on Chapter 6, isn't it unusual for CEOs to say they regret their initial misguided approach to a tool like the NPS? It's not unusual for David Tudehope or members of his leadership team – it's just authenticity and honesty.

Practice your magic

1. In what ways is your department or business "so unlike" competitors? How do you leverage those differentiating characteristics to attract prospects?
2. What false choices are you making? Where can you demonstrate ambidexterity and pursue two seemingly dichotomous objectives?
3. How do you provide "direct service" to customers?
4. In what ways do you serve customers by helping them help themselves?
5. How do you demonstrate a genuine interest in and appreciation for customers?
6. What is the role of gift-giving in your organization?
7. Does your department or business operate from scarcity or abundance? How comfortable are you with sharing your best practices?

Approachability and authenticity

You have experienced David Tudehope admitting that he initially launched a failed gift-giving program. Based on my experience, those examples reflect behavior that is rare in most businesses. Being approachable, giving one's time, and acknowledging errors continue to be off the beaten path for many leaders. But, as Charlene Li writes in the *Harvard Business Review*, "Business and leadership is all about relationships. In any relationship, things go wrong, mistakes are made, and ups are followed by downs. The strength of a relationship is not how perfect it is, but how resiliently it deals with the inevitable failures."

Accordingly, leadership approachability, authenticity, and humility drive strong and resilient employee relationships at Macquarie. Josh Dominguez, a Cybersecurity Analyst, notes:

> "I came from a large and very impersonal employer where I couldn't imagine looking in the eyes of the CEO, let alone talking to him. However, David Tudehope and the entire leadership have taken an interest in me from early in the recruiting process. My Macquarie journey started when a team member contacted me on LinkedIn, followed by a technical interview with our hiring manager, Naveen Gera. I then met with the head of operations, Tony Pandher, followed by James Mystakidis, Group Executive for Cloud Services. Not only did these leaders spend time with me, but they focused on my needs, explained the Macquarie culture, and helped me feel comfortable that Macquarie was right for me. About half an hour of my time with James was spent talking about movies and cars. I was shocked that senior leaders would take that much time getting to know me for an entry-level position. Since then, I have had countless lunches or dinners with senior leaders, including our CEO."

Similarly, Kayal Vili Manamohan, a Macquarie Service Delivery Manager, shares:

> "I went through many interviews coming out of college, and Macquarie stood out. The Macquarie

> selection process was the only time I felt valued and valuable. Unlike all other companies, Macquarie executives were involved throughout the process and showed a genuine interest in me. They asked me what I wanted from a career at Macquarie. They listened intently, acknowledged my goals, showed me how they would help me grow, and emphasized the impact I could have on Macquarie's customers and my community."

Kayal adds that she continues to experience the genuine interest of leaders:

> "I have regular meetings with managers and executives on operational issues and my career path. As my two-year contract was coming to an end, my manager suggested I consider a position as a Service Delivery Manager. That suggestion came from an understanding of my strengths and interests. I was surprised by the option since no one had made that career move at Macquarie. Usually, engineers advance to more technical roles, but I wanted to help customers with operational issues."

As a Service Delivery Manager, Kayal works with her customer base as part of a Macquarie team that includes an Account Executive and a Personal Customer Technical Officer (PCTO). The Account Executive oversees sales, the PCTO focuses on technical needs, and Kayal builds relationships by understanding the customer's technology environment and ensuring their operations run smoothly. Kayal adds, "My role is a perfect fit for me, and leaders are helping me explore certifications and training resources for this first-of-a-kind transition. I am eager to shape this path so others have it as an established option."

Dan Morgan, a Macquarie Personal Customer Technical Officer, suggests that Macquarie's "road less traveled" leadership approach involves more than spending time with or expressing interest in team members:

> "Leaders at Macquarie understand and empathize with the challenges team members face. Most of them have been in our shoes, and they understand that our jobs are rewarding but challenging. By sharing their stories and insights, they inspire us to do the same for new team members coming on board. Leaders also share the pitfalls and mistakes they've made along the way. Those stories permit us to take calculated risks for our customers."

Dan's words are consistent with findings shared by the University of Houston Professor and leadership researcher Brené Brown in a Netflix special titled *Brené Brown: The Call to Courage*: "No vulnerability, no creativity. No tolerance for failure, no innovation. It is that simple. If you're not willing to fail, you can't innovate. If you're unwilling to build a vulnerable culture, you can't create."

Practice your magic

1. Generally, how willing are leaders in your organization to admit mistakes and shortcomings? How willing are you to do the same?

2. How present and engaged are managers and leaders in your organization? How do they appear unexpectedly (e.g., early in a selection process, at onboarding or through informal interactions)?

3. Besides being accessible, to what degree do leaders demonstrate their genuine interest in team members? How do they show that interest?

4. To what degree does your department or company demonstrate a "vulnerable culture," showing it is safe to take risks and innovate?

5. How can you increase healthy vulnerability, accessibility, and genuine interest at work?

Translating trust into impact

Team members at Macquarie suggest that leaders serve as role models when it comes to taking calculated risks intended to improve the lives of colleagues and customers. That role modeling also demonstrates that sometimes risks don't produce optimal results. Even then, lessons can be learned to guide further improvement. Cybersecurity Analyst Josh Dominguez notes, "I'm empowered to use costly equipment to solve complex customer problems. Macquarie's leaders have created an environment where I rely on my experience and the experience of team members to creatively tackle problems and not worry about building the perfect solution."

Personal Customer Technical Officer Dan Morgan shows how customers and team members benefit from feeling safe to innovate:

> "Another Macquarie team previously got stuck trying to tailor a solution for a customer to back up a huge, non-standard, legacy file server consisting of important banking and financial records. Observing the process, I used my free time to consider possible options. Having wrestled with the issue intermittently for about a week, I had an idea for modifying how we deployed the software for the backup. I remember patterning with the customer and our team and seeing my idea work. The customer was elated. I felt incredibly fulfilled, and the other Macquarie engineers were extremely grateful. Not every solution turns out this way, but I will remember that one for a long time."

David Tudehope sums up his company's zig-zag journey this way:

> "Macquarie was created because telecom customers were treated as subscribers, and monopolies and oligopolies were increasing prices yearly. We recognized the opportunity to change this for business and government customers. We remain relevant by looking for other markets where business and government customers are underserved and overcharged and where we can make this same difference. We aren't making business decisions to drive conformity or build a moat around us. We function to improve the lives of people in the businesses we serve so they can best serve people in our communities. As a leader at Macquarie, I must show up for our people, acknowledge my mistakes, celebrate our victories, and share

what we've learned. That way, Macquarie sustains its lasting impact, and our people understand that zigging when others zag means we serve when others underserve."

Make your difference

- It's easy to market yourself as unconventional. However, to be credible with that message, you must develop repeatable processes that separate your business from others (e.g., studying the actions of competitors and considering vastly different ways to achieve customer success).
- Groupthink is real. Its antidote is to seek data to inform decisions and to encourage contrarian views.
- In business, leaders are often willing to make "false choices." They choose one path over the other even when journeying on both paths is best.
- According to Professor Michael L. Tushman, managers need to create ambidextrous organizations that balance stability and incremental change on the one hand and experimentation and discontinuous change on the other.
- Leaders can operate from abundance or scarcity. Those who operate from abundance share their insights and best practices freely and attract colleagues who do the same.
- Admitting mistakes is not a sign of leadership weakness; those admissions set the stage for strong and resilient cultures.
- While people typically think of service as involving "direct action," service can also include assisting others in helping themselves, spending time with those you serve, and acknowledging others personally.

- Service recovery must first resolve the customer's issue. Later in the process, gift-giving can be helpful to acknowledge or offset the customer's inconvenience.
- Professor Brené Brown said, "If you're not willing to build a vulnerable culture, you can't create."
- From David Tudehope's perspective, zigging when others zag means elevating your service and value delivery when others underserve and overcharge.

Chapter 9

Looking to the Future with Macquarie's Magic

"Show the world your magic."
Torian Salary

Macquarie has been challenging the seemingly impossible for 30 years.

To put that timeline in a technology context, Macquarie started a year before Amazon, two years before the first handheld device (the PalmPilot), five years before Google, eight years before the iPod, ten years before the Android, and eleven years before Facebook. Macquarie has also outlasted the rise and fall of such brands as Netscape, BlackBerry, AltaVista, and Napster. In short, 30 years is an eternity in the technology industry, where the journey from hero to zero can happen in only a couple of years.

Unfortunately, as the US Securities and Exchange Commission requires mutual funds to say, "past performance does not necessarily predict future results." Since this book has heavily spotlighted Macquarie's strengths, I will offer a counterbalance by sharing the company's vulnerabilities (most of which apply to any business in a growth or maturity stage), starting with talent selection and development.

The ability to find and develop talent

While all companies compete in the war for talent, Macquarie's hiring profile – "humble, hungry, and smart" people who are "enthusiastically human and technically literate" – significantly narrows their qualified candidate pool. Social, educational, and workplace changes make talent selection and development especially difficult for Macquarie.

Naveen Gera, Head of Service Assurance, explains:

> "Over the past few years, we've noticed changes in workplace preparedness among recent graduates. Socialization and collaboration issues surfaced when universities shifted to online learning in response to pandemic lockdowns. Our new graduates were technically competent but hadn't had the opportunity to be in rooms with peers to hash out technical problems. I now have new hires sitting next to one another and texting back and forth, instead of getting up and heading to a conference room to innovate a solution on a whiteboard. Also, candidates respond differently when I tell them they must work tirelessly for their first two years at Macquarie and that their short-term sacrifices will pay off over their careers. Unfortunately, many people today aren't ready, willing, or able to make such a substantial commitment."

Luke Clifton, Group Executive for Macquarie Telecom, notes, "Overall, the telecom industry here in Australia has under-invested in its talent pool for a long time. Our competitors' reliance on outsourcing to places like the Philippines and India has hollowed out our industry. This makes our investment in training and development especially important."

For Macquarie to sustain success, leaders must select from a pool of team members who place immersive career development at or near the top of their priorities. Leaders at Macquarie will also need to address any socialization gaps that emerge from reduced in-person educational experiences and sustain focus on differentiating themselves as an employer of choice through career development offerings.

Managing growth

While I don't have a crystal ball to tell me Macquarie's future growth curve, Conor O'Prey, Senior Industrials Analyst at Canaccord Genuity Group suggests Macquarie is poised for sizable growth in the foreseeable future: "Based on current expansion plans, Macquarie will likely enjoy sizable near-term growth surges, followed by more longer-term growth."

As Macquarie's Data Centre footprint increases, the company will likely also experience growth in its Cloud Service business. Given those likely increases and a growing need for cybersecurity services in government and non-government settings, Macquarie is well-positioned for sustained growth. So, will leaders at Macquarie be able to scale in accord with demand? Conor O'Prey says yes:

"As you look at Macquarie's progression and its developed assets, you'll see the company has been getting steadily and incrementally bigger. This has happened even though leaders haven't taken massive swings for the fence. Instead, they've been incredibly deliberate in driving and managing growth. For example, if you look at the compound EBITDA growth rate of Macquarie since 2003, it is roughly 18 or 19 percent. If you look at the growth rate from 2021 to 2022, it is almost identical. So, Macquarie's trajectory has been very consistent, and scaling isn't something I would worry about for this company since the way leaders have run the business has earned them the market's confidence that the business has the potential to continue to grow bigger."

Figure 7: Macquarie's growth

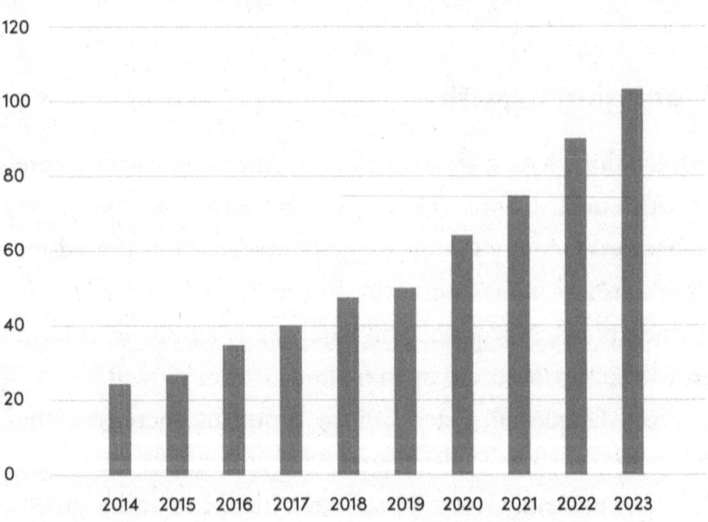

Sustaining the purpose-driven culture

To sustain success, Macquarie must maintain its purpose-driven culture and continue differentiating itself through service and value creation. Conor O'Prey agrees:

> "Macquarie has a clear service differentiator reflected in a Net Promoter Score of around 79. From my perspective, that type of NPS suggests that customers are extremely happy and willing to recommend Macquarie to colleagues. Hypothetically, if Macquarie were sitting at an NPS of 30, customer churn would be higher and revenue growth would be lower. In turn, the company would probably have to employ more people in its sales departments to find new customers to offset the churn. Therefore, not only would its revenue be lower but costs would be higher. Thus, profits would decline. As such, Macquarie needs to maintain its service differentiation in a sector known for miserable experiences."

To maintain its outstanding employee and customer experience culture, Macquarie must maintain its investments in people and positive storytelling (initiatives like the Heartbeat program). It must continue its disciplined approach to translating customer insights into action (through tools like the NPS). Leaders will periodically need to refresh messages about the importance of customer experience so those messages hold team members' attention. Macquarie's reward and recognition programs may also need to be tweaked to continually reignite the pursuit of human experience excellence (for colleagues and customers).

Making the right big bets and staying entrepreneurial

To ensure sustained future success, Macquarie's leaders must continue to make sound innovation investments. Those investment decisions will likely involve sustained deployment and refinement of Macquarie's Noah's Ark approach to innovation study tours.

Macquarie's co-founder Aidan Tudehope notes:

> "Because innovation is the lifeblood of our industry, we have taken and will continue to take a disciplined approach to infuse and sustain the same entrepreneurial spirit that led David and me to launch this business decades ago. Our innovation tours also serve as a repeatable process for assessing new opportunities and determining which significant future investments will meet the needs of, and be embraced by, the markets we serve."

Former Starbucks CEO Howard Schultz used to describe his business's significant investments as "the few big future bets that we seldom can afford to lose." Macquarie's leadership team and board of directors must also steer the company away from the choppy waters of hubris and complacency that many mature brands encounter. They must stay hungry and avoid becoming the very thing Macquarie challenged – a legacy brand ripe for disruption.

Business author Jim Collins writes about how and why companies grow, plateau, and decline. Having authored a breakthrough book titled *Good to Great: Why Some Companies Make the Leap... and Others Don't* (in which he featured category-leading brands), Jim noticed that many of his featured brands lost their luster or relevance after the book's publication. In a brief preview to a subsequent book, *How the Mighty Fall: And Why Some Companies Never Give In*, Jim outlined the five stages of business decline, which he referred to as hubris born of success, the undisciplined pursuit of more, denial of risk and peril, grasping for salvation, and capitulation to irrelevance and death.

According to Jim, the seeds of decline are sown through denial of risk and complacency, as evidenced by a concept Jim refers to as "Bill Gore's waterline principle." Jim explains, "If you blow a hole above the waterline (where the ship won't take on water and possibly sink), you can patch the hole, learn from the experience, and sail on. But if you blow a hole below the waterline, you can find yourself facing gushers of water pouring in, pulling you toward the ocean floor." The story's moral is, don't get reckless or cocky and incur damage from which you can't recover.

In keeping with Jim Collins's cautionary wisdom, Group Executive David Hirst notes:

> "History tells us that any company that thinks and behaves like they are number one stops innovating, becomes arrogant and blows up their business. So, culturally, we must always act like we are number two, striving to be number one. That's the only way to sustain world-class performance."

Conor O'Prey is not worried about Macquarie's leadership becoming complacent or making faulty choices:

> "David and Aidan Tudehope have a multi-decade record of steadily guiding Macquarie and making necessary pivots. For example, when you compare Macquarie's 2009 annual report to the present day, you will see how the company's revenue streams have evolved because leaders positioned the company

> ahead of market shifts. In 2009, Macquarie's telecom business generated the bulk of the company's revenue compared to what was then called 'hosting,' now data center revenue. Fast forward to the present, and telecom and data center business revenue have completely flipped. Both quantitatively and qualitatively, Macquarie has ensured that the company addresses the right market segments at the right times, which gives me confidence that Macquarie's leaders will be able to do so."

Conor's assessment notwithstanding, Macquarie leaders must remain "humble, hungry, and smart."

Shifting from founder-led to founder-inspired

One of Macquarie's greatest strengths – sustained co-founder leadership – may be one of its most significant long-term vulnerabilities. Someday, the company will need to transition from what the leadership support team at Spencer Stuart calls a "founder-led" to a "founder-inspired" company. To successfully navigate the eventual retirement of its founders, Chris Zook and James Allen, authors of *The Founders Mentality: How to Overcome the Predictable Crises of Growth*, suggest companies like Macquarie must transfer a founder's mindset to future generations of leaders.

Specifically, Zook and Allen note, "Since 1990, we've found that the return to shareholders in public companies where the founder is still involved is three times higher than in other companies . . . The most significant high performers exhibit the attributes of the founder's mentality four to five times more than the worst performers." They attribute this to the loss of the founder's mentality that occurs as companies become larger and more organizationally complex, with more processes and systems, a diluted sense of insurgency and increased difficulty in maintaining the original talent level.

In their book, Zook and Allen visually depict this profound shareholder return, illustrated here in Figure 8.

Figure 8: Founder-led companies consistently outperform

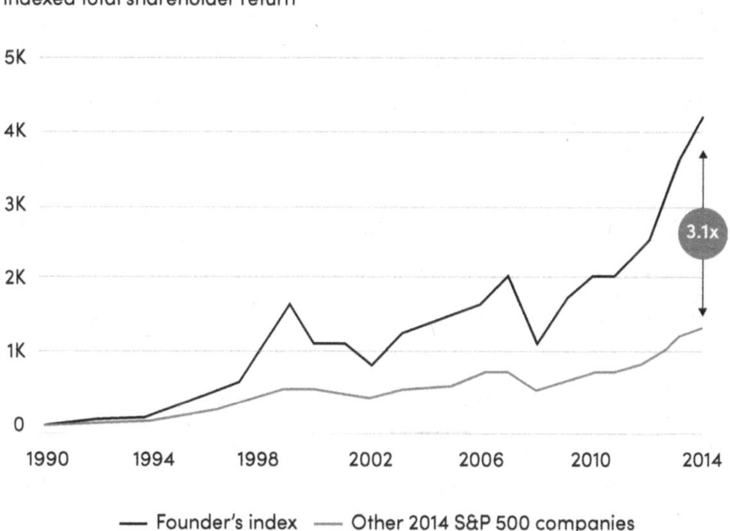

Reprinted with permission from "Founder-Led Companies Outperform the Rest – Here's Why" by Chris Zook. Mar 24, 2016, hbr.org. Copyright 2016 by Harvard Business Publishing.

To ensure the founder's mentality extends beyond the direct leadership of the founders, Zook and Allen suggest that companies like Macquarie focus on an insurgent mission, spikiness (a continual emphasis on what makes a business unique), and a limitless time horizon.

From the onset of Macquarie, David, and Aidan crafted

and have maintained a company-wide focus on "making a difference for markets that are underserved and overcharged." This approach epitomizes how Zook and Allen define an insurgent mission: "waging war against an industry on behalf of underserved customers."

The key for Macquarie will be to keep the company's purpose alive well past David and Aidan's direct leadership. Similarly, future generations of leaders must maintain an unwavering focus on Macquarie's unique differentiators (spikiness) and drive the belief that Macquarie has a limitless timeline. This means they must have confidence that Macquarie's core success will enable the company to successfully provide solutions that meet adjacent and emerging customer needs.

James Mystakidis, Group Executive, notes:

"We are well aware of the challenges companies have faced when it comes to maintaining the founder's mindset. We are also students of Zook and Allen's work. To that end, we have intentionally focused on driving our founders' insurgent mindset, spikiness, and limitless timeline across our leadership team and inculcating it throughout our organization. I am confident our founders' mindset will thrive long past the direct involvement of David and Aidan."

Naveen Gera also believes the values and vision of Macquarie's co-founders are deeply engrained across the company:

> "I hope David and Aidan don't step down from Macquarie for a long time because we will inevitably experience a loss. However, I've been fortunate to be a part of this business for over ten years and have learned much from them. As a hiring manager, I

recruit and onboard new team members. It is a privilege to share what David and Aidan shared with me. So, suppose in another decade, David and Aidan decide their work at Macquarie is done. In that case, their imprint on the culture, commitment to making a difference, and legacy will live through our next generation of leaders."

Senior Industrials Analyst at Canaccord Genuity Group Conor O'Prey provides an outsider's perspective:

> "I've been covering Macquarie for over five years, and throughout that time, its executive team has been extremely stable. More importantly, when I watched the group interact, I saw a vibrant debate with David, its CEO, sitting back and not imposing his will. In those interactions, all leaders have had the opportunity to be heard and to challenge one another's ideas. The founders have shaped the Macquarie culture while enabling leaders to grow and develop to provide the company with the talent pipeline to give the business the best chance to succeed if or when a team member is called to move up in the founder's absence."

Enough about Macquarie's potential pitfalls. Based on my time with leaders, managers, and frontline team members, I am convinced that Macquarie leaders regularly and objectively assess strengths, weaknesses, opportunities, and threats. As such, they will navigate challenges wisely and continue to produce Macquarie magic by challenging the seemingly impossible.

Performing your magic

Professional magicians adhere to a code of conduct: never share your secrets – unless, of course, it's with other professional magicians. Since you are a fellow customer experience and innovation creator, Macquarie leaders have freely shared their secrets with you. They and I hope you will use insights from this book to enhance your service magic.

B. Joseph Pine and James H. Gilmore, pioneers in customer experience design and delivery, and authors of the groundbreaking book *The Experience Economy: Work Is Theater and Every Business a Stage*, emphasize the importance of thinking about customer experience delivery in the context of a stage performance (like a magic show) – but not just in terms of entertainment. The authors note that at every level, "companies stage an experience whenever they engage customers, connecting them in a personal and memorable way . . . the resulting experience, rich with sensations created within the customer . . . lingers in the memory of any individual engaged in the event."

Similarly, customer experience thought leader Scott McKain observes, "No matter what your organization does. No matter what your distribution channels are. No matter what services you offer or what products you manufacture . . . YOUR business is show business."

Given this context, let's get on with your show.

It is time to take the stage

Since you will invite an audience (prospective and existing customers) to your magic show, you must be clear about what magic you plan to perform. How will you benefit your audience through your ability to master a "seemingly impossible" challenge? How will you make your customers' lives easier, better, or more successful through your product or service delivery?

Once your unique value proposition is clear, you'll need to craft a statement that describes the vision and the values-based behavior required for a successful performance. You'll then need to surround yourself with frontstage and backstage team members who understand your vision and find value in pursuing it. Those colleagues should be selected based on talent and personality characteristics to guarantee your audience receives that magic you've promised. What vision will you share with prospective crew members, and what hiring guidelines will you use to bring together your optimal team?

For your team to work effectively together, you must rehearse all performance elements and seek input from those participating in or attending your early shows. As you master your craft, you will continue to invite audience feedback and use that input to polish rough spots and innovate new offerings. You will also need to remind yourself and your team that your shows may become routine to you, but each performance may be a one-of-a-kind experience for your customer.

But that's down the road. Tonight is opening night!

The stage is set, and you hear the chatter and energy of the audience through the closed curtain. You take a breath to remind yourself of the purpose that guides your performance. The frontstage and backstage crews are collaborating flawlessly. The stage lights come up, the curtains open, and you confidently step centerstage to perform your unique customer experience and innovation magic.

Here's to rave reviews, repeat visits, word-of-mouth referrals, standing-room-only audiences, and the privilege of making a lasting difference for those you serve.

About the Author

Joseph A. Michelli, Ph.D., C.S.P., is an internationally sought-after speaker, author, and organizational consultant who transfers his knowledge of exceptional business practices in ways that develop joyful and productive workplaces with a focus on customer experience. His insights encourage leaders and frontline workers to grow and invest passionately in all aspects of their lives. Dr Michelli is a *Wall Street Journal*, *USA Today*, *Publishers Weekly*, *Nielsen BookScan*, and #1 *New York Times* bestselling author. His books include *The Starbucks Experience*, *The New Gold Standard*, *Prescription for Excellence*, and *The Airbnb Way*. Global Gurus has named him one of the Top 5 Customer Experience thought leaders for six consecutive years.

References

Chapter 1 – Macquarie's Customer Magic

Telecommunications Industry Ombudsman, *Annual Report 2018-19*, n.d., tio.com.au/reports/annual-report-2018-19.

The Australian Communications Consumer Action Network (ACCAN), "Can you hear me? Ranking the customer service of Australia's phone and internet companies," 23 July 2018, accan.org.au/media-center/hot-issues-blog/1525-can-you-hear-me-ranking- the-customer-service-of-australia-s-phone-and-internet-companies.

Telecommunications Industry Ombudsman, "Annual report 2018: phone and internet companies turning a corner," 17 October 2018, tio.com.au/reports/annual-report-2018-phone-and-internet-complaints-turning-corner.

Best Places to Work, "Best Places to Work Winners: Macquarie Telecom Group," accessed 10 August 2023, afrbestplacestowork.com/past-winners/macquarie-telecom

Chapter 2 – David (and Aidan) Against Goliath

Ross, P, "The deregulation of the Australian telecommunications sector: workforce restructuring and employment relations (ER) at Telstra in a deregulated environment," *Proceedings of the 18th Association of Industrial Relations Academics of Australia and New Zealand (AIRAANZ) Conference*, 2004.

Neville, A, "The pros and cons of sibling partnerships," *Forbes*, 27 September 2013, forbes.com/sites/amandaneville/2013/09/27/the-pros-and-cons-of-sibling-partnerships.

"Interview: telco founder reveals his "Noah's Ark" strategy for success," *Fear & Greed*, podcast, 28 February 2022, fearandgreed.com.au/2022/02/28/interview-telco-founder-reveals-his-noahs-ark-strategy-for-success.

Hendricks, B, Howell, T & Bingham, C, "Research: how long should a founder remain CEO?", *Harvard Business Review,* 17 December 2021, hbr.org/2021/12/research-how-long-should-a-founder-remain-ceo.

The Oxford Dictionary of Quotations, 4th ed., Oxford University Press, Oxford, UK, 1992.

Covey, SMR, *The Speed of Trust: The One Thing That Changes Everything*, Free Press, New York, 2006.

Dweck, C, "What having a "growth mindset" actually means," *Harvard Business Review*, 13 January 2016, hbr.org/2016/01/what-having-a-growth-mindset-actually-means.

Chapter 3 – From Purpose to Culture

Messana, P, "What is company culture?", *Forbes*, 11 March 2022, forbes.com/sites/forbestechcouncil/2022/03/11/what-is-company-culture/?sh=b4c0dd3279be.

Schulze, H & Merrill, D, *Excellence Wins: A No-nonsense Guide to Becoming the Best in a World of Compromise*, Zondervan, Grand Rapids, USA, 2019.

National Geographic Society, "Storytelling and cultural traditions," *National Geographic*, updated 3 December 2022, education.nationalgeographic.org/resource/storytelling-and-cultural-traditions.

Coyle, D, *The Culture Playbook: 60 Highly Effective Actions to Help Your Group Succeed*, Cornerstone, 2022.

Chapter 4 – It's Always About the People

Lencioni, PM, *The Ideal Team Player: How to Recognize and Cultivate the Three Essential Virtues*, John Wiley & Sons, New York, 2016.

Pennington, S, "Call center jobs . . . dead end or tech career stepping stone?", *The Sydney Morning Herald*, 13 May 2014, smh.com.au/technology/call-center-jobs--dead-end-or-tech-career-steppingstone-20140512-zrag5.html.

Chapter 5 – Seeking Freedom Within Boundaries

Pink, DH, *Drive: The Surprising Truth About What Motivates Us*, Riverhead Books, New York, 2009.

Reichheld, FF, *The Ultimate Question 2.0: How Net Promoter Companies Thrive in a Customer-driven World*, Harvard Business Review Press, Boston, 2011.

"Gallup's Employee Engagement Survey: Ask the Right Questions with the Q12® Survey," *Gallup*, accessed 14 June 2023, gallup.com/ workplace/356063/gallup-q12-employee -engagement-survey.aspx.

Lambert, N, "How Empowering Your Employees Helps Improve Business," *Huffpost*, 11 December 2017, huffpost. com/entry/howempowering-your-employees-helps -improve-business_b_5a2eec0ee 4b0bad787126f08.

Chapter 6 – The Art and Science of World-class Customer Experience Delivery

Pemberton, C, "Key findings from the Gartner Customer Experience Survey," *Gartner*, 16 March 2018, gartner.com/ en/ marketing/insights/articles/key-findings-from -the-gartner-customer-experience-survey.

"U.S. overall customer satisfaction," *American Customer Satisfaction Index*, accessed 14 June 2023, theacsi.org/ the-acsi-difference/us-overall-customer-satisfaction.

Reichheld, FF, "The one number you need to grow," *Harvard Business Review*, December 2003, hbr.org/2003/12/the-one-number-you-need-to-grow.

Gocheva, C, "Telecommunications NPS benchmarks and CX trends – Updated September 2021," *Experience Benchmarks*, accessed 20 November 2021, customergauge.com/benchmarks/ blog/telecommunications-nps-benchmarks-and-cx-trends.

Chapter 7 – A Noah's Ark of Innovation

Thomke, S & Randal, J, "The magic of innovation," *The European Business Review*, 21 May 2014, europeanbusinessreview.com/magic-innovation.

Gross, D, *Forbes Greatest Business Stories of All Time*, Wiley, New York, 1997.

Hamel, G, "Bringing Silicon Valley inside," *Harvard Business Review*, September–October 1999, hbr.org/1999/09/bringing-silicon-valley-inside.

Chapter 8 – Zigging when Others Zag

Mueller, J, Harvey, S & Levenson, A, "How to steer clear of groupthink," *Harvard Business Review*, 7 March 2022, hbr.org/ 2022/03/how-to-steer-clear-of-groupthink.

Stebbins, P, "My leadership fails: group think disasters," *LinkedIn*, 10 August 2015, linkedin.com/pulse/my-leadership-fails-group-think-disasters-dr-pete-stebbins.

Li, C, "The art of admitting failure," *Harvard Business Review*, 28 March 2011, hbr.org/2011/03/the-art-of-admitting-failure. *Brené Brown: The Call to Courage*, video, Netflix, 2019.

Chapter 9 – Looking to the Future with Macquarie's Magic

Collins, J, *Good to Great: Why Some Companies Make the Leap . . . and Others Don't*, Random House Business Books, London, 2001.

ibid., "How the mighty fall: a primer on the warning signs," *Jim Collins*, May 2009, jimcollins.com/books/how-the-mighty-fall.html.

Baumgarten, J, Caswell, LJ, Charlesworth, S & Frangos, C, "Transitioning from founder-led to founder-inspired: best practices for the board," *Spencer Stuart*, April 2022, spencerstuart.com/research-and-insight/transitioning-from-founder-led-to-founder-inspired.

Zook, C & Allen, J, *The Founder's Mentality: How to Overcome the Predictable Crises of Growth*, Harvard Business Review Press, Boston, 2016.

Pine, BJ & Gilmore, JH, *The Experience Economy: Work Is Theatre and Every Business a Stage*, Harvard Business School Press, Boston, 1999.

McKain, S, *ALL Business Is STILL Show Business: Create Distinction and Earn Standing Ovations from Customers in a Hyper-competitive Marketplace*, CreateSpace Independent Publishing Platform, 2017.

Index